PIP BREAST IMPLANTS

The Essential Guide

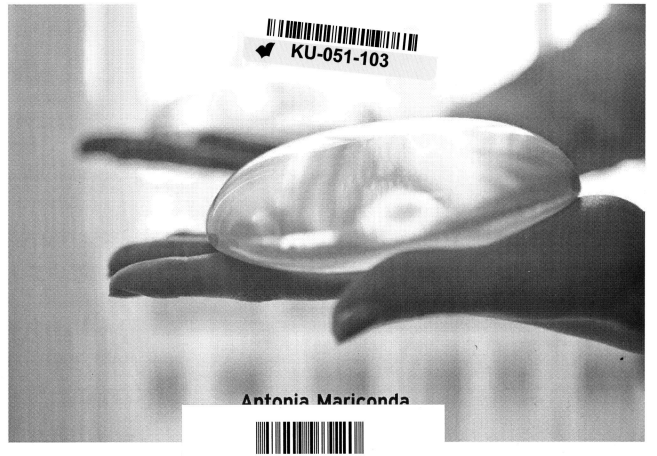

Antonia Mariconda

Breast Surgery and PIP Implants – The Essential Guide is also available in accessible formats for people with any degree of visual impairment. The large print edition and eBook (with accessibility features enabled) are available from Need2Know. Please let us know if there are any special features you require and we will do our best to accommodate your needs.

First published in Great Britain in 2012 by
Need2Know
Remus House
Coltsfoot Drive
Peterborough
PE2 9BF
Telephone 01733 898103
Fax 01733 313524
www.need2knowbooks.co.uk

Contents

Introduction

Between the years 2001 and 2009, about 80,000 Poly Implant Prothèse (PIP) implants – representing some 40,000 women – were sold in the UK.

It is estimated that between 2,000 and 3,000 of these implants were used by the National Health Service (NHS).

The majority of the remainder were used by the major Cosmetic Surgery Groups in the UK (including The Harley Medical Group, Transform and The Hospital Group) as well as other smaller providers and clinics.

From about 2006 onwards, concerns began to emerge among cosmetic surgeons in the UK about the performance of PIP implants. The alarm was originally raised after many patients and surgeons reported premature rupturing.

Implants are designed to last a minimum of ten years, however the lifespan of PIP implants was averaging at as little as just three years.

This guide is written with the purpose of assisting you and giving you factual advice and information on all forms of breast surgery and PIP implants.

If you do not know what type of implants you have had, or you have had confirmation that you currently have PIP implants, you may be worried about some of the reports that you have read, therefore you will be wanting to read some information to give you guidance and reassurance.

This informative guide consists of two parts, these will give you:

- Information on breast surgery and help you understand the various types of surgery associated with the breasts.
- A background history and overview as to what Poly Implant Prothèse (PIP) is and how PIP implants came to be in the UK.
- Information on diagnosing whether you have PIP implants.
- Choices that you can consider if you have PIP implants.
- The costs and considerations of surgery associated with PIP implants.

- Emotional support and advice on legal issues.
- Answers to frequently asked questions.
- Advice in find a reputable surgeon.

Whatever your situation is be reassured that there is good advice and help currently available through a number of organisations listed in the help list.

Disclaimer

This book is for general information only about breast surgery and PIP implants. It is not intended to replace professional medical advice, although it can be used alongside it. Anyone with PIP implants or who suspects that they have PIP implants should seek medical advice from a health-care professional, such as their GP, in the first instance

The author, Antonia Mariconda, also known as The Cosmedic Coach, is recognised as a leading authority on health, beauty and cosmetic surgery in the UK. Quoted in publications such as *Top Santé*, and newspapers such as *The Evening Standard*, and *Daily Mail*, Antonia's name and face are familiar in the world of cosmetic surgery, beauty and anti-ageing.

Antonia is a national health and beauty writer and the Author of *Acne – The Essential Guide, Foot Care – The Essential Guide* (Need2Know), and most notably *The Cosmetic Surgery Companion – Look and Feel Beautiful* (Apple Press)

As The Cosmedic Coach, Antonia advises clients around the world on where to shop safely for cosmetic surgery, beauty and anti-ageing treatments.

With thanks

To the medical associations listed within this book and the kind organisations that assisted in the writing of this information.

Part 1
Breast Surgery

Chapter One

Plastic and Cosmetic Surgery of the Breast

Understanding the difference between cosmetic surgery and plastic surgery

Just because the name includes the word 'plastic' doesn't mean patients who have this surgery end up with a face full of fake stuff. The name isn't taken from the synthetic substance but from the Greek word 'plastikos', which means to form or mould (and which gives the material plastic its name as well).

Plastic surgery is a special type of surgery that can involve altering both a person's appearance and ability to function. Plastic surgeons strive to improve patients' appearance and self-image through both reconstructive and cosmetic procedures.

Reconstructive procedures

Reconstructive procedures correct defects on the face or body. These include physical birth defects like cleft lips and palates and ear deformities, traumatic injuries like those from dog bites or burns, or the aftermath of disease treatments like rebuilding a woman's breast after surgery for breast cancer.

Cosmetic procedures

Cosmetic (also called aesthetic) procedures alter a part of the body that the person is not satisfied with. Common cosmetic procedures include making the breasts larger (technically known as augmentation mammoplasty) or smaller (technically known as reduction mammoplasty), reshaping the nose (technically known as rhinoplasty), and removing pockets of fat from specific spots on the body (technically known as liposuction).

Some cosmetic procedures aren't even surgical in the way that most people think of surgery – that is, cutting and stitching. For example, the use of special lasers to remove unwanted hair or to smooth the skin to improve severe scarring are two such treatments, these are often referred to as non-surgical cosmetic procedures.

'Plastic surgery of the breast is one of the most popular areas of cosmetic plastic surgery.'

What is plastic surgery and cosmetic surgery of the breast?

Plastic surgery of the breast is one of the most popular areas of cosmetic plastic surgery. Last year, according to the annual audit of the British Association of Aesthetic Plastic Surgeons (BAAPS), over 10,000 breast procedures were carried out. This represents only a fraction of the true amount of surgical breast procedures carried out in the United Kingdom, as not all plastic and cosmetic surgeons working in the UK are registered members of the BAAPS, so the figure is estimated to be more than triple.

Plastic surgery of the breast includes several different breast surgery procedures.

These include:

- Breast enlargement, technically referred to as 'breast augmentation' which is usually accomplished with breast implants.

- Breast lift (technically referred to as 'mastopexy') which is a procedure that is often performed simultaneously with a breast augmentation.

In addition to these purely cosmetic procedures, there is also:

- Breast reduction (technically described as a 'reduction mammoplasty') which is an enhancement surgery that potentially offers both health and cosmetic benefits.

- Breast reconstruction is often another breast surgery procedure required after breast mastectomy.

Understanding the different types of breast surgery

There are currently several types of breast surgery operations available, these include:

Breast augmentation

A breast augmentation, also known as breast enlargement, is surgery to increase the size of the breasts or correct asymmetrical breasts. It usually involves placing an artificial breast implant filled with silicone (cohesive gel that doesn't run if cut) or saline (saltwater) either under the breast tissue or the chest muscle behind the breast.

Breast enlargement implants are available in a variety of shapes, forms and sizes. A breast implant can be made of natural body tissue or synthetic (manmade) materials, such as saline breast implants or silicone breast implants. Natural tissue breast enlargement implants are usually only used on women having breast reconstruction surgery (after breast cancer treatment) and are rarely used for cosmetic purposes.

Breast reconstruction

Breast reconstruction is an operation to try to get back the shape of the breast after mastectomy (removal of a breast), or lumpectomy (removal of part of the breast) as a result of a cancer. The aim of a breast reconstruction operation is to match the remaining natural breast as closely as possible. This can either be done by creating a breast 'form' with a breast implant, or by using natural tissue from another part of the body. If a person has lost one or both breasts, the creation of a new breast can dramatically improve their self-image, self-confidence and quality of life. However, although breast reconstruction surgery can give a person a relatively natural-looking breast, a reconstructed breast will never look or feel exactly the same as the breast that was removed. Breast reconstruction typically involves several procedures performed in multiple stages. It can begin at the same time as mastectomy (the surgical removal of a breast), or a person may choose to delay this stage until they have healed from a mastectomy operation and recovered from any additional cancer treatments.

Breast reduction

Breast reduction is a cosmetic surgery procedure that lifts the breast and makes it smaller. Women with large breasts often suffer from back pain, neck pain, breast pain and other medical problems, and breast reduction surgery will help to relieve the symptoms. For this reason, it is considered a reconstructive surgery and is often covered by insurance. During the breast reduction operation, excess tissue and skin are removed from the breasts. The breasts are then reshaped to form smaller ones, and the nipples are repositioned.

Breast lift

Breast lift is an operation to raise and reshape the breasts if the breasts have lost their shape and skin elasticity through pregnancy, breastfeeding, or as a result of a loss or gain in weight, or simply due to natural gravity as part of the ageing process. There are several different techniques that can be used in a breast lift procedure, depending on the degree of skin that needs to be surgically manoeuvred.

Breast implant revision

Breast implant revision, also referred to as breast augmentation revision or breast revision, is a cosmetic surgery procedure involving the removal and/or replacement of breast implants to correct complications that have occurred after breast augmentation or implant-based breast reconstruction surgery. Breast implant revision can also be performed to correct an unsatisfactory result from either of the surgeries mentioned.

You will find out about all these different procedures in more detail in the following chapters.

Why women seek breast plastic surgery

Women seek breast surgery for a number of reasons; the main reasons are because:

- They are genetically disposed to smaller breasts.

- They are genetically disposed to breasts that are not symmetrical or a 'tubular' shape, with one breast having a different size or shape than the other, this is also known as 'asymmetrical' breast correction.

- Breast cancer patients often seek breast reconstruction surgery because a breast is partially or totally removed as part of the cancer treatment.

- Of reduced firmness from ageing.

- Of drooping or sagging breasts after child bearing and breastfeeding (this condition most often, requires two procedures: breast lift and breast augmentation).

Whether your breasts are too large, too small or not as firm or as shapely as you would like, breast surgery is one way to help make you feel more confident and feminine again.

In general, a prospective ideal candidate for breast plastic surgery is:

- 18 years of age or older.

- Not currently pregnant or nursing.

- In good physical health.

- Psychologically stable.

- Wanting to improve their appearance.

- Realistic in their expectations.

'. . . breast surgery is one way to help make you feel more confident and feminine again.'

※ Fully informed of the risks and benefits, physical and financial, in the short, medium and long term.

Find out about the procedure

Read as much as you can about the procedure that you are considering. You need to be sure that it is right for you and that you understand exactly what is involved, including any risks, side effects and possible complications. Make sure that the information is from a reliable source.

The Department of Health provides information on more than 100 different types of surgical and non-surgical cosmetic procedures. It also gives a detailed checklist of questions to ask the clinic and doctor before deciding. See the help list for information.

'Read as much as you can about the procedure that you are considering. You need to be sure that it is right for you and that you understand exactly what is involved.'

Summing Up

- Last year, according to the British Association of Aesthetic Plastic Surgeons (BAAPS), over 10,000 breast procedures were carried out in the UK, though due to the fact that not all plastic and cosmetic surgeons are registered members of the BAAPS, it is estimated this figure could be triple.

- Breast surgery is carried out for both cosmetic and non-cosmetic reasons.

- There are several different types of breast surgery operations available, including: breast augmentation, breast reduction, breast reconstruction, breast lift and breast implant revision.

- Breast surgery procedures can improve self-confidence and change the way you look and feel about your image and appearance.

Chapter Two

Breast Augmentation

Breast augmentation (augmentation mammoplasty) is one of the most common breast surgery procedures. Women have many different reasons for choosing to undergo breast augmentation surgery. Most women choosing to have breast augmentation operations want to improve their self-esteem and self-image, and a breast augmentation procedure can help to improve their appearance and increase their self-confidence.

Implant options

Breast augmentation implants are available in a variety of shapes, forms and sizes. A breast implant can be made of natural body tissue or synthetic (manmade) materials, such as saline breast implants or silicone breast implants. Natural tissue implants are usually only used on women having breast reconstruction surgery (after breast cancer treatment) and are rarely used for cosmetic purposes.

Breast implants generally do not tend to last a lifetime. If you decide to have a breast enlargement, you may well need at least one additional surgery on your breasts over your lifetime, for example if the breast implants break down or rupture; other complications (for example breast pain); or if the breasts are asymmetrical, of an unsatisfactory size, or if there is wrinkling/rippling of the breasts. The possible future financial cost of further breast implant surgery (breast revision) must also be taken into account.

The first major step towards getting breast implants is to schedule a breast augmentation consultation. During a consultation with a surgeon you should be prepared to ask your most important questions, preparation and research leads to a more satisfying experience.

'Most women choosing to have breast augmentation operations want to improve their self-esteem and self-image.'

Discussion of your personal goals: size, shape and implant options

A consultation for breast augmentation will include discussion about the type of breast implant that is most appropriate for you. There are many shapes, sizes and materials of breast implant from which to choose. Your surgeon will be able to recommend the best choice for you based on your body type, contour and amount of change that you desire.

How is a breast augmentation procedure performed?

The following demonstrates how breast augmentation operations are usually carried out, though individual surgical practice may vary.

Step 1 – Anaesthetic

Breast implant operations are usually carried out under general anaesthetic, though sometimes your surgeon will use intravenous sedation. Your surgeon will recommend the best choice for you. It is possible to have a breast augmentation operation as day surgery, though you will normally need to stay in hospital overnight. Breast augmentation usually takes about one to three hours to complete. The length of the procedure varies according to the technique used, the placement of the implants, the patient's anatomy, and type of anaesthesia used.

Step 2 – Types of incision

Your doctor will first make an incision, or cut, in an inconspicuous area to minimise visible scarring. You will be able to discuss these options with your doctor before your operation to decide on the one that is best for you. Incisions vary based on the type of breast implant, degree of enlargement desired, your anatomy, and where you would like the scars to be.

Incision options include:

- Inframammary – a small cut is made in the fold beneath each breast.

- Transaxillary – a cut is made in your armpit, and may cause more visible scarring than the other types of incision.

- Periareolar – this incision, made around the nipple, causes only minimal scarring, though there is a possibility that nipple sensation may be affected.

- Transumbilical – breast implants are implanted by first going through an incision of the belly button area. A thin instrument is inserted into the belly button area, which later inserts the saline implant.

After the incision has been made, the implant is inserted either beneath the breast tissue (sub-mammary/sub-glandular) or under the pectoral muscle (sub-muscular). Again, your surgeon will advise you on the best option. The cuts are then closed using fine stitches which may be dissolvable, and your breasts are wrapped in a special supportive dressing or support bra. You may also need to have drainage tubes fitted for up to 48 hours, to help drain away excess fluids.

Step 3 – Results

The results of your breast augmentation procedure will be immediately obvious. While most women are pleased with how they look, they are not always as happy with how their breasts feel. You may have numbness in your nipple area which is a common complication, or your breasts may feel supersensitive and painful to the touch. Your breasts may remain swollen and sensitive to physical contact for a month or longer, though over time the swelling subsides and the incision lines will refine and fade.

When you wake up you will feel tired, sore and stiff, and you will be advised to take painkillers. Post-operative care may involve the use of a post-operative bra, compression bandage, or a jog bra for extra support and positioning while you heal.

Your breasts will be wrapped with gauze bandages as well as a tighter bandage for protection and support after your breast implant surgery. Someone will need to drive you home, and you may need assistance over the next couple of days. Before you leave the hospital, you and whoever is caring

'The results of your breast augmentation procedure will be immediately obvious.'

for you post-op will be given instructions on the symptoms you may experience, and the possible complications of which to be aware. It is very important to take the medication prescribed to you by your surgeon.

Breast augmentation recovery and healing steps

Breast augmentation surgery is usually carried out under general anaesthetic and therefore has the same risks as other invasive surgical procedures; any kind of surgical procedure carries a small risk of infection.

It takes a few months for the breasts to settle after surgery and in the short term patients might experience some swelling, hardness and discomfort with some bruising, twinges and pains possibly over the first few weeks. The combination of increased volume from the breast implant and swelling from surgery may cause your breasts to feel large, heavy and tight. While in the hospital, you will be encouraged to rest in an upright position to help reduce swelling.

'Your scars will be pink for several weeks, but after several months they will begin to fade.'

Depending on the size of the breast implant and the way it was placed during surgery, some mild bruising may occur. Rarely, this bruising can extend down to the abdomen. While this is uncommon, it is not considered a complication. However, if you have any large, firm, painful areas of bruising, contact your doctor. This may be a haematoma, which is a more serious type of bruise and will need treatment. Normal bruising should subside in one to two weeks.

Post-surgery, you will be given pain relief if you are in pain. Your scars will be pink for several weeks, but after several months they will begin to fade.

You may need to stay in the hospital overnight, or you may be allowed home the same day. It is critical that you follow your doctor's guidance and advice on post-operative care. You will normally need to attend a number of post-operative check-ups to ensure that you are recovering well.

Follow these steps to help to ensure a speedy and healthy breast implant recovery:

- Rest – Get as much as possible following your procedure. Drink plenty of fluids, and be sure to take the doctor's prescribed medications. Avoid sleeping on your front for one month.

- Avoid lifting your arms – For at least three to five days, you should try to keep arm extension to a minimum. The tissues will heal more quickly if you avoid stretching and separating muscle/tissue surrounding the breast implants.

- Take it easy – Avoid physical exertion for several weeks and driving for one week. You should be able to return to work two to four weeks after your breast enlargement procedure, depending on the advice of your doctor. Breast implant recovery times vary from patient to patient and depend upon the technique, type of implant and site of placement that the doctor uses, as well as the level of activities in your daily routine.

- Keep dry – Avoid getting water on your wounds for a week.

Breast enlargement recovery times vary for individuals; it is a gradual process, you must be aware that you need to get help if any of the following occur to you.

If you suffer from any of the following, tell your surgeon or nursing staff immediately:

- Excessive swelling.

- Deflated breasts.

- Offensive-smelling wound discharge.

- A fever of 38°C (106°f) or more.

- Excessive pain or burning heat in your breast.

Breast augmentation side effects and risks

Breast implant procedures are commonly performed and generally safe. However, in order to make an informed decision and give your consent, you need to be aware of the possible side effects and the risk of complications.

Side effects

These are the unwanted, but mostly temporary, effects of a successful treatment, for example, feeling sick as a result of the general anaesthetic.

For a few weeks after surgery, your breasts will feel sore, swollen and hard, and you will feel a burning sensation in your nipples. Using extra pillows when sleeping can help reduce the swelling around your breasts.

You will have scars, they will be pink and noticeable at first, but they should fade gradually.

Summing Up

▨ Most women who undergo breast augmentation are doing so to improve their self-image and self-esteem.

▨ Breast implants generally do not last a lifetime, therefore the possibility of future surgery and costs should be taken into account before having the operation.

▨ The surgeon will advise on the best choice of implant that is most appropriate for your body type, contour and the amount of change desired.

▨ Breast augmentation surgery carries the same risks as any other surgical procedure.

▨ There are many issues to take into consideration before undergoing breast augmentation, for example the possibility that any surgical changes carried out on your breasts may be both undesirable and irreversible.

Chapter Three

Breast Reconstruction Surgery

Breast reconstruction is a type of surgery for women who have had a breast removed (mastectomy). The surgery rebuilds the breast so that it is about the same size and shape as it was before. The nipple and the darker area around the nipple (areola) can also be added. Most women who have had a mastectomy can have reconstruction. Women who have had only the part of the breast around the cancer removed (lumpectomy) may not need reconstruction. Breast reconstruction is done by a plastic surgeon.

Up to 47,700 women are being diagnosed every year with breast cancer, equal to 130 a day. That is double the number 30 years ago. Today, the emotional and physical results are very different from what they were in the past. Much more is now known about breast cancer and its treatment. New kinds of treatment as well as improved reconstructive surgery mean that women who have breast cancer today have better choices.

Today, more women with breast cancer choose surgery that removes only part of the breast tissue. This may be called breast conservation surgery, lumpectomy, or segmental mastectomy. But some women have a mastectomy, which means the entire breast is removed. Many women who have a mastectomy choose reconstructive surgery to rebuild the shape and look of the breast.

Women choose breast reconstruction for many reasons:

- To make their breasts look balanced when they are wearing a bra.

- To permanently regain their breast shape.

▓ So they don't have to use a form that fits inside the bra (an external prosthesis).

Several types of operations can be done to reconstruct your breast. You can have a newly shaped breast with the use of a breast implant, your own tissue flap, or a combination of the two. (A tissue flap is a section of your own skin, fat and muscle which is moved from your tummy, back or other area of your body to the chest area.)

The stages of breast reconstruction surgery

One-stage immediate breast reconstruction may be done at the same time as mastectomy. After the general surgeon removes the breast tissue, a plastic surgeon places a breast implant where the breast tissue was removed to form the breast contour.

'One-stage immediate breast reconstruction may be done at the same time as mastectomy.'

Two-stage reconstruction or, two-stage delayed reconstruction, is done if your skin and chest wall tissues are tight and flat. An implanted tissue expander, which is like a balloon, is put under the skin and chest muscle. Through a tiny valve under the skin, the surgeon injects a saltwater solution at regular intervals to fill the expander over time (about 4 to 6 months). After the skin over the breast area has stretched enough, a second surgery is done to remove the expander and put in the permanent implant. Some expanders are left in place as the final implant.

The two-stage reconstruction is sometimes called delayed-immediate reconstruction because it allows options. If the surgical biopsies show that radiation is needed, the next steps may be delayed until after radiation treatment is complete. If radiation is not needed, the surgeon can start right away with the tissue expander and second surgery.

Implant procedures

The most common implant is a saline-filled implant. It is a silicone shell filled with saltwater (sterile saline). Silicone gel-filled implants are another option for breast reconstruction. They are not used as often as they were in the past because of concerns that silicone leakage might cause immune system diseases. But most of the recent studies show that silicone implants do not increase the risk of immune system problems. Also, alternative breast implants that have different shells and are filled with different materials are being studied, but you can only get them in clinical trials.

Tissue flap procedures

These procedures use tissue from your tummy, back, thighs or buttocks to rebuild the breast. The two most common types of tissue flap surgeries are the TRAM flap (or transverse rectus abdominis muscle flap), which uses tissue from the tummy area, and the latissimus dorsi flap, which uses tissue from the upper back.

These operations leave two surgical sites and scars – one where the tissue was taken and one on the reconstructed breast. The scars fade over time, but they will never go away completely. There can also be problems at the donor sites, such as abdominal hernias and muscle damage or weakness. There can also be differences in the size and shape of the breasts. Because healthy blood vessels are needed for the tissue's blood supply, flap procedures are not usually offered to women with diabetes, connective tissue or vascular disease, or to smokers.

In general, flap procedures behave more like the rest of your body tissue. For instance, they may enlarge or shrink as you gain or lose weight.

'In general, flap procedures behave more like the rest of your body tissue. For instance, they may enlarge or shrink as you gain or lose weight.'

TRAM (transverse rectus abdominis muscle) flap

The TRAM flap procedure uses tissue and muscle from the tummy (the lower abdominal wall). The tissue from this area alone is often enough to shape the breast, and an implant may not be needed. The skin, fat, blood vessels, and at least one abdominal muscle are moved from the belly (abdomen) to the chest. The TRAM flap can decrease the strength in your belly, and may not be possible in women who have had abdominal tissue removed in previous surgeries. The procedure also results in a tightening of the lower belly, or a 'tummy tuck'.

There are 2 types of TRAM flaps:

- A pedicle flap leaves the flap attached to its original blood supply and tunnels it under the skin to the breast area.

- In a free flap, the surgeon cuts the flap of skin, fat, blood vessels, and muscle for the implant free from its original location and then attaches it to blood vessels in the chest. This requires the use of a microscope (microsurgery) to connect the tiny vessels and takes longer than a pedicle flap. The free flap is not done as often as the pedicle flap, but some doctors think that it can result in a more natural shape.

Latissimus dorsi flap

The latissimus dorsi flap moves muscle and skin from your upper back when extra tissue is needed. The flap is made up of skin, fat, muscle and blood vessels. It is tunnelled under the skin to the front of the chest. This creates a pocket for an implant, which can be used for added fullness to the reconstructed breast. Though it is not common, some women may have weakness in their back, shoulder or arm after this surgery.

DIEP (deep inferior epigastric artery perforator) flap

A newer type of flap procedure, the DIEP flap, uses fat and skin from the same area as in the TRAM flap, but does not use the muscle to form the breast mound. This results in less skin and fat in the lower belly (abdomen), or a 'tummy tuck'. This method uses a free flap, meaning that the tissue is completely cut free from the tummy and then moved to the chest area. This requires the use of a microscope (microsurgery) to connect the tiny vessels. The procedure takes longer than the TRAM pedicle flap discussed previously.

Gluteal free flap

The gluteal free flap or SGAP (superior gluteal artery perforator) flap is a newer type of surgery that uses tissue from the buttocks, including the gluteal muscle, to create the breast shape. It is an option for women who cannot or do not wish to use the tummy sites due to thinness, incisions, failed tummy flap, or other reasons. The method is much like the free TRAM flap mentioned on page 27. The skin, fat, blood vessels, and muscle are cut out of the buttocks and then moved to the chest area. A microscope (microsurgery) is needed to connect the tiny vessels.

New methods of tissue support

These surgeries move sections of tissue to new places, or add fairly heavy implants, and some tissues need support to keep them in place as they heal. Doctors use synthetic mesh and other methods for this. More recently, doctors are trying a new product made of donated human skin (AlloDerm®). It is regulated by the US Food and Drug Administration (FDA) as a human tissue used for transplant. But it has had the human cells removed (known technically as being 'acellular'), which reduces any risk that it carries diseases or the body will reject it. It is used to extend and support natural tissues and help them grow and heal. In breast reconstruction it may be used with expanders and implants. It has also been used in nipple reconstruction.

This product is fairly new in breast reconstruction. Studies that look at outcomes are still in progress, but have been promising. AlloDerm® is not used by every plastic surgeon, but is becoming more widely available.

Summing Up

- Breast reconstruction is a type of surgery for women who have had a mastectomy (a breast removed as part of treatment for breast cancer).

- One-stage immediate breast reconstruction can be done at the same time as a mastectomy is carried out.

- Two-stage delayed reconstruction is carried out over a period of months where stages of the procedure can be delayed to allow for any necessary treatment to be completed, e.g. radiotherapy.

- If you are thinking about having reconstructive surgery, it is a good idea to talk about it to a plastic surgeon experienced in breast reconstruction before your mastectomy. This lets the surgical teams plan the treatment that is best for you, even if you want to wait and have reconstructive surgery later.

- Breast reconstruction is done using either an implant procedure or a tissue flap procedure. The most common implant surgeons use is a saline-filled one. Alternatively, with a tissue flap procedure, tissue from the stomach, back, thighs or buttocks is used to rebuild the breast.

Chapter Four

Breast Reduction Surgery

A breast reduction is also known technically as reduction mammoplasty, this is a surgical procedure that brings the breasts into better proportion with the rest of the body by removing fat, excess breast tissue and skin. The areola, or darker skin around the nipple, may be reduced and repositioned as well.

Large breasts can dominate a woman's appearance and give an unbalanced physical profile and make exercise difficult or even impossible to do. Breast reduction surgery is a procedure for reshaping exceptionally large breasts surgically to increase comfort and satisfaction. Overly large breasts frequently have a considerable affect on self-confidence and can even affect personal relationships. The aim of surgery is to give you smaller, shapelier breasts that are in proportion to the rest of your body.

For numerous women, it's not just the aesthetic issues they want to address in considering a surgical breast reduction, for many it is also about feeling physically better, as many women (and men) experience problems associated with overly large breasts such as back pain, neck pain, and skin irritations, to even more serious issues like skeletal deformations and breathing problems. One of the most common problems comes from bra straps. They're pushed to the limit and that means indents in your skin. All of these lead to being self-conscious about your body.

Some breast reduction procedures are carried out in tandem with a breast lift procedure. A breast reduction and lift is an ideal choice for women who wish to improve the shape and the position of their breasts. Some women also desire an increase in volume and size, and so breast implants may be inserted in conjunction with a breast lift.

Breast lift procedures are also appropriate for younger women as well who wish to address asymmetrical breast correction.

'The aim of surgery is to give you smaller, shapelier breasts that are in proportion to the rest of your body.'

Breast reduction surgery procedure steps

Breast reduction operations are usually performed through incisions made on your breasts with the surgical removal of the excess fat, glandular tissue and skin.

In some cases, excess fat may be removed through liposuction in conjunction with the excision techniques described below. Breast size is largely due to fatty tissue and excess skin is not a factor, liposuction alone is not used for breast reduction.

The technique used to reduce the size of your breasts will be determined by your individual condition, breast composition, amount of reduction desired, your personal preferences and the individual plastic surgeon's advice.

Step 1 – Anaesthesia

Medications are administered for your comfort during the surgical procedure. The choices include intravenous sedation and general anaesthesia. Your doctor will recommend the best choice for you.

Step 2 – The incision

Incision options include:

- A circular pattern around the areola.
- A keyhole or racquet-shaped pattern with an incision around the areola and vertically down to the breast crease.
- An inverted T or anchor-shaped incision pattern.

Step 3 – Removing tissue and repositioning

After the incision is made, the nipple – which remains tethered to its original blood and nerve supply – is then repositioned. The areola is reduced by excising skin at the perimeter, if necessary.

Underlying breast tissue is reduced, lifted and shaped. Occasionally, for extremely large pendulous (sagging) breasts, the nipple and areola may need to be removed and transplanted to a higher position on the breast (free nipple graft).

Step 4 – Closing the incisions

The incisions are brought together to reshape the now smaller breast. Sutures are layered deep within the breast tissue to create and support the newly shaped breasts; sutures, skin adhesives and/or surgical tape close the skin. Incision lines are permanent, but in most cases will fade and significantly improve over time.

Step 5 – See the results

The results of your breast reduction surgery are immediately visible. Over time, post-surgical swelling will resolve and incision lines will fade. The incision lines that remain are visible and permanent scars, although usually well concealed beneath a swimsuit or bra. Satisfaction with your new image should continue to grow as you recover.

Breast reduction surgery recovery and healing steps

'The incision lines that remain are visible and permanent scars, although usually well concealed beneath a swimsuit or bra.'

▧ After you awake and are taken into the recovery room following your breast reduction surgery, the recovery nurse will monitor your vital stats until you are ready to be released. This is dependent upon the individual but may take up to two hours or more. You will feel quite tender and possibly confused as the anaesthesia wears off.

▧ A drain may be inserted to allow the fluids an exit from the incision sites or from the bottom most portion of the treatment area. You will be swollen and bruised and will more than likely be wearing a type of compression garment or surgical bra with elastic bandages binding your breasts to your body.

▧ It is important that you keep your incisions/suture line dry. Your breast reduction surgeon may have placed Steri-Strips on top of your incision line and sutures, or you may have internal sutures and tissue glue externally to bind your incision edges. Either way your surgeon will give you specific care instructions.

- You will have your incision sites checked and your stitches removed in approximately 10 days.

- Whilst you are healing from breast reduction surgery, take your temperature regularly. An elevated temperature could mean an infection.

- Pain tolerances depend upon the individual, but you will feel tender, stiff and sore for a few days and will more than likely not want to move too much. This will subside. Be sure to take your required medications and follow the precise instructions provided to you by your surgeon.

- As with all surgeries, swelling will be an issue. Swelling is a normal reaction to an injury and is categorised as a natural inflammatory action.

- You may be swollen for up to 3 to 4 months, although this could be very slight and only noticed by you. Your breasts, of course, will be smaller than they were before, and higher, so you may not notice swelling too much, perhaps just soreness.

- Bruises may or may not be present after your surgery. This depends entirely on the patient.

- Sleeping can be difficult initially, it is important to sleep with at least 2 to 3 fluffy pillows under your upper back and head to keep your torso elevated. This helps relieve pressure on your treatment area, reducing swelling and pain.

- Even though you may not feel like it, your surgeon will more than likely advise you to walk and move around as soon as you are able. If you do not and you lie around, you may develop clots and or retain fluid (swelling, oedema) a lot longer.

- You will most likely be instructed not to exercise or engage in strenuous activities for at least 3 to 4 weeks. Breast reduction recovery times vary for each individual. Take your time in healing so that you give yourself the best healing environment possible.

Breast reduction side effects and surgery risks

While breast reduction surgery, when performed by an experienced and qualified plastic surgeon, often has pleasing results, there are a number of breast reduction side effects you will have to prepare for after the surgery. Usually, they are not of a serious nature. However, you should prepare for a period of several months to make a complete recovery from your breast reduction surgery.

Talk to your surgeon in detail about the potential risks, benefits and possible complications of breast reduction surgery before you commit to having the procedure performed. The prognosis is highly dependent upon your individual circumstances, and the advice of a qualified medical professional should be taken very seriously.

Be aware that permanent scarring cannot be avoided when a patient undergoes breast reduction surgery. While skilled doctors can do an excellent job of hiding and masking the scarring, and it will be hidden when wearing a bra or bathing suit, it will be present to some degree.

Prepare to face post-surgical pain. While this can typically be managed through the use of prescription drugs, the pain following a reduction mammoplasty surgery can sometimes be severe and may necessitate a corrective surgical procedure.

Discuss the possibility of breast asymmetry with your surgeon during your initial consultations. Breast asymmetry results when, after a breast reduction procedure, one breast remains slightly larger than the other.

Be aware that all breast reduction procedures carry a considerable risk that the woman will lose the ability to breastfeed. This is because most of the milk ducts in the breast are removed or otherwise altered during the surgical procedure. If your ability to breastfeed is important to you, a breast reduction may not be the right choice.

In rare cases, some (if not all) of the feeling in your breasts and/or nipples, can be lost, even after you are fully healed. While skilled, experienced surgeons are usually able to avoid damaging the blood vessels that nourish the breast nerve endings, there are no guarantees.

'Be aware that all breast reduction procedures carry a considerable risk that the woman will lose the ability to breastfeed.'

Summing Up

▓ Breast reduction (also known as reduction mammoplasty) is a surgical procedure that removes fat and excess breast tissue and skin.

▓ The aim of the surgery is to reduce the size of breasts and bring them into better proportion with the rest of the body.

▓ Some breast reduction procedures are performed in conjunction with a breast lift, for women who wish to improve the shape and position of their breasts.

▓ All breast reduction procedures carry the risk that the patient may lose the ability to breastfeed.

▓ Permanent scarring cannot be avoided, and will always be present to some degree.

Chapter Five

Breast Lift Surgery

Over time, a woman's breasts often change, many factors can bring about a loss of youthful shape and firmness to the breasts, and loss of skin elasticity. These causes include: pregnancy, breastfeeding, weight fluctuations and weight gain, ageing and natural gravity; heredity and genes also have a lot to answer for. Sometimes a woman in her teens may experience loose, sagging breast tissue due to simple genetic heredity. Breasts that have lost their once firm uplifted contours can have a negative effect on a woman's self-confidence and self-image. A breast lift – technically known as a mastopexy – is a surgical procedure whereby a plastic surgeon restructures breasts that have lost their original shape and appear to have an element of sagging or loss of volume to them.

A breast lift procedure raises and firms the breasts by removing excess skin and tightening the surrounding tissue to reshape and support the new breast contour. Sometimes the areola (the pigmented skin surrounding the nipples) can become enlarged over time; a breast lift will reduce this appearance as well. Where an increase in volume and size is desired, breast implants may also be inserted in conjunction with a breast lift.

Breast lift procedures are also appropriate for women as well who wish to address asymmetrical breast correction.

Breast lift surgery procedure steps

A breast lift without implants is a highly individualised procedure achieved through a variety of incision patterns and techniques. The appropriate technique for your individual case will be determined on your breast size and shape, the size and the position of your areola, the degree of your breast sagging, and your skin quality and skin elasticity as well as the amount of extra skin.

Step 1 – Anaesthesia

Medications are administered for your comfort during the surgical procedures. The choices include intravenous sedation and general anesthesia. Your doctor will recommend the best choice for you.

Step 2 – The incision

The incision pattern for a breast lift will be determined based on individual breast size and shape, excess skin and skin elasticity of the individual patient in order to achieve realistic goals.

The incision may include a circle around the areola, a line extending down the lower portion of the breast from the areola to the crease underneath the breast and a line along the crease of the breast.

Not every patient will require all of the incisions mentioned. It is possible to perform a breast lift through an incision around the areola only, or through a combination of incisions around the areola and a vertical incision down the lower portion of the breast.

Most commonly, three incisions, including one along the breast crease, are used. The combination length and extent of incisions depends on the amount of excess skin to be removed and the quality of the skin.

Once the excess skin is removed, the breast tissue is reshaped and lifted and the remaining skin tightened as the incisions are closed.

Some incisions resulting from a breast lift are concealed in the natural breast contours; others are visible on the breast surface.

Non-removable sutures are layered deep within the breast tissue to create and support the newly shaped breasts; sutures, skin adhesives and/or surgical tape may be used to close the skin

Incision lines are permanent but in most cases fade and improve significantly with time.

Step 3 – Results

The results of breast lift surgery are immediately visible. Over time post-surgical swelling will subside and resolve, and incision lines will gradually refine in appearance. Patients experience an immediate satisfaction at their results, and experience fulfilment in self-confidence and personal body image in achieving their goal for an uplifted breast profile.

Breast lift surgery recovery and healing

Once your breast lift procedure is completed, the surgical areas will be covered in dressing or bandages and an elastic bandage or support bra will be given to the patients to wear. The purpose of a support bra or bandage is to minimise swelling and support the breasts as they heal, you may have to wear a support bra for the first week or two.

Breast lift recovery times vary from patient to patient. Initial breast lift recovery may include swelling and slight discomfort at the incision sites and in breast tissue overall. It is quite common to experience discomfort and this can be controlled with medication.

Your medical team will advise you of:

* How to care for the breasts following surgery, and the importance to cleanse the incision sites and apply any ointment as directed, and it is important you follow that advice carefully, as this is essential to the success of your final outcome.

* Medications to apply or to take orally to reduce the risk of infection.

* Specific changes at the surgical site or in overall health.

* Follow-up consultations with your breast lift surgeon.

A return to light and normal activity is possible as soon as you feel ready, which is normally a few days after surgery, however initial wound healing may take between 5 to 10 days, at which time any sutures will be removed.

'Patients experience an immediate satisfaction at their results, and experience fulfilment in self-confidence and personal body image in achieving their goal for an uplifted breast profile.'

You will be able to return to work and resume normal activity after this time. It is advisable not to engage in any vigorous exercise or activity or heavy lifting within 4 to 6 weeks after your procedure.

Breast lift recovery times can take up to several weeks as swelling slowly resolves and implant position settles. Incision lines will gradually fade; although they remain permanent they are often inconspicuous.

Breast lift side effects and surgery risks

The decision to have breast lift surgery is an exceptionally personal one, and you will have to decide if the surgery will achieve your goals and expectations. Risks and potential complications are possible and it is advised that you discuss these in detail with you breast lift surgeon.

Breast lift procedures are commonly performed and generally safe. However, in order to make an informed decision and give your consent, you need to be aware of the possible side effects and the risk of complications.

Breast lift side effects

These are the unwanted, but mostly temporary, effects of a successful treatment, for example, feeling sick as a result of the general anaesthetic.

For a few weeks after surgery, your breasts will feel sore, swollen and hard, and you will feel a burning sensation in your nipples. Using extra pillows when sleeping can help reduce the swelling around your breasts.

You will have scars, they will be pink and noticeable at first, but they should fade gradually.

It's possible that you still won't be satisfied with your appearance after the operation.

Breast lift risks

- Unfavourable scarring.
- Bleeding (haematoma).

- Infection.

- Poor healing of incisions.

- Changes in nipples or breast sensation – may be temporary or permanent.

- Skin discoloration, pigmentation changes, swelling and bruising.

- Damage to deeper structures such as nerves, blood vessels, muscles and lungs – may be temporary or permanent.

- Breast asymmetry.

- Fluid accumulation.

- Excessive firmness of the breast.

- Potential partial or total loss of the nipple or areola.

- Blood clots.

- Deep vein thrombosis, cardiac and pulmonary complications.

- Pain.

Summing Up

- Breast lift surgery is performed to restructure breasts that have lost their original shape. The procedure raises and firms the breasts by removing excess skin and tightening the surrounding tissue.

- Breast lift surgery can also be used to correct asymmetrical breast problems.

- As with all breast surgery procedures, breast lift surgery carries a number of risks and side effects, including infection, possibility of damage to nerves and muscles, and asymmetry.

Chapter Six

Breast Implant Revision

Breast implant revision is also referred to as breast augmentation revision or breast revision, this is a cosmetic surgery procedure involving the removal and/or replacement of breast implants to correct complications that have occurred after breast augmentation or implant-based breast reconstruction surgery. Breast implant revision can also be performed to correct an unsatisfactory result from either of the surgeries mentioned.

There are many reasons why a patient will need implant revision or replacement. The most common reasons for breast implant revision surgery are usually implant leakage or rupture, capsular contracture and a change in size or shape.

Am I a candidate for breast implant revision surgery?

Patients who are discontented with the results of their previous breast implant surgery may be candidates for a revision. Some women experience unwelcome complications after breast augmentation, such as asymmetry, breast pain, implant deflation, and other side effects. Fortunately, it is possible to correct most aesthetic and medical complications with the removal or replacement of implants.

'Fortunately, it is possible to correct most aesthetic and medical complications with the removal or replacement of implants.'

How is a breast implant removal and replacement procedure performed?

For implant removal surgery, general anaesthesia or intravenous sedation is normally used. An incision is made either around the areola or under the fold of the breast. The capsule around the implant is cut into and the implant is carefully removed. If the implant is silicone-filled, it is inspected for any signs of damage and rupture before removal. If the implant is filled with saline, the surgeon may choose to deflate the implant to help removal. The implants are then replaced with new ones. The scar tissue (capsule) that was around the implant may also be removed (if the implant is not going to be replaced).

If the surgical procedure consists only of removing the old implants, then pain will be minimal. If implants and capsules are removed, the discomfort will be similar to the discomfort experienced after a standard breast augmentation procedure.

You should be pain-free until the day after your surgery. If you experience some discomfort, prescription pain medication will be available to you. You may be asked to take antibiotics and other medications as necessary.

Breast implant removal and replacement surgery side effects and surgery risks

Like all surgical procedures, with breast implant removal surgery there is always a possibility of complications. Although these complications are extremely rare, they can include:

- Infection.
- Adverse reaction to anaesthesia.
- Excessive bleeding.
- Unsatisfactory results.

Breast asymmetry may occur after breast implant removal surgery if implants are not replaced. It is important to bear in mind that you may be disappointed with the results of breast implant removal surgery. Additional surgery may be necessary to reshape breasts after implant removal.

Some patients require no further breast surgery after their breast implants have been removed, while others may require a breast lift. Some breast lifts may be extensive while others may be very limited. Breast lift surgery can leave scars on the outside of breasts, which will heal in time.

If the implant shell has been damaged or ruptured, it may be impossible to remove all of the escaped gel from the surrounding tissues. This is a particular problem if the surrounding scar capsule, which usually contains the leaked gel, has also been injured or damaged.

It is not possible to predict with certainty how a woman will look after implant removal surgery. Much depends on the nature of the scar capsule and whether the implant has ruptured.

Breast implant removal and replacement surgery recovery and healing

Recovery and healing times do vary from patient to patient. Your stitches would normally be removed 5-7 days post-surgery, bruising subsides gradually over the course of 2-3 weeks. You should walk around the house with some assistance. Every day, walk around the house, slowly increasing your level of activity. Avoid raising your shoulders above 90 degrees for 2 weeks, for instance to reach a plate high in the cupboard. If you have small children try and arrange for their care by your spouse or another guardian for the first few days. You will need to avoid reaching or lifting of any kind for at least a week and for as long as two weeks. Although it is important to keep the breast area clean throughout the healing process to avoid infections, breast implant removal patients should not submerge their incisions in a bath, swimming pool or other body of water until the breasts have completely healed. Avoid touching the incisions or bringing any product, such as lotion or deodorant, into contact with the stitched area. You should be able to return to work after a week. However, if your job requires physical activity, you should wait two weeks before resuming a full workload. It may take your body up to six weeks to make

'It is not possible to predict with certainty how a woman will look after implant removal surgery.'

a full recovery. As your body heals during that time, you will gradually regain strength of movement. Your scars may take up to seven months to completely heal.

Summing Up

- Breast implant revision is a cosmetic surgery procedure carried out to remove or replace breast implants, and to correct complications that have occurred after breast augmentation or implant-based surgery.

- Breast implant revision can also be performed to correct an unsatisfactory outcome from a previous breast surgery procedure.

- Additional surgery may be necessary to reshape the breasts after breast implant revision, as breast asymmetry may occur.

Chapter Seven

Breast Implant Facts and Advice Before Surgery

A breast implant is a medical prosthesis used to correct the size and form of a woman's breasts in post-mastectomy breast reconstruction; for correcting congenital defects and deformities of the chest wall; and most commonly for aesthetic breast augmentation.

There are three general types of breast implant device, defined by the filler material: saline, silicone, and composite.

- The saline implant has an elastomer silicone shell filled with sterile saline solution.

- The silicone implant has an elastomer silicone shell filled with viscous silicone gel.

- The alternative composition implants feature miscellaneous fillers, such as soy oil, or polypropylene string.

In 1961, the American plastic surgeons Thomas Cronin and Frank Gerow, and the Dow Corning Corporation, developed the first silicone breast prosthesis filled with silicone gel; in due course, the first augmentation mammoplasty was performed in 1962 using the Cronin-Gerow Implant, prosthesis model 1963. In 1964, the French company Laboratoires Arion developed and manufactured the saline breast implant, filled with saline solution, and then introduced it for use as a medical device in 1964.

What qualifies a safe breast implant?

Anyone wanting breast augmentation needs to to do their homework and find a reputable plastic surgeon that is a member of local or international bodies. The quality of silicone implants in general has significantly reduced the risk of rupture, rippling and capsular contracture. The FDA (The Food and Drug Administration) has officially ruled that breast implants are safe, with identified complications such as leaking, rupturing or scarring occurring rarely.

Understanding the difference between a CE marked breast implant and an FDA-approved breast implant

The only approval necessary for a medical device to become instantly available across Europe is a CE mark (Conformité Européenne) – the very same CE mark used for toys and mobile phones. For medical devices, the CE mark need only be granted by just one of 74 notifying bodies authorised in 25 countries in the EU. Once a device is CE marked, any variations to its design or the materials used can be waved through without scrutinisation.

That's what happened with PIP breast implants. Following CE approval the company dropped a protective outer skin, lowered the silicone grade – and weren't legally required to inform any official body in Europe.

The US Food and Drug Administration is the only global independent regulatory body for medical devices that has had a 100% success rate in identifying which breast implants are not up to standards. Their stringent regulatory testing processes take an average of 54 months to complete versus the EU's 11 months.

The EU applies the CE marking process primarily to ensure safety, as well as a reinforced manufacturer obligation with respect to device claims. The FDA does this too, but has the additional constraint of evaluating efficacy, which is indirectly but ultimately linked to health-care reimbursements. In other words, both systems are set up to ensure patient/user safety and to enforce a device does what it says it's meant to do, with the FDA looking at the wider picture and asking 'Does healthcare really need this?'

How do I know a breast implant is safe?

The FDA decided that breast implants are 'reasonably safe' for most women for the three years that were studied, but unfortunately saline implants were not studied for long-term safety.

'Reasonably safe' does not mean safe for everyone. The FDA found that most implant patients have at least one serious complication within three years after getting their silicone or saline implants. Breast pain, breast hardness and numbness in the nipple are common complications that may last for years, and may never go away.

Many breast augmentation patients need additional surgery within 5 years of getting breast implants. Within 10-12 years, most women will need at least one additional surgery.

It is unpredictable how long an implant will last. Some implants break within a few days, weeks, or months, while others last for many years.

Like most new products, most implants seem fine for the first few years. Think of implants as being as reliable as a car – problems can happen anytime, but the older they get, the more problems you are likely to have.

The FDA found that by the time a woman has implants for 10 years, at least one of them has broken. However, it is not always obvious.

All breast implants have the same basic design. Implants are made up of a silicone envelope, with a filling of some kind – usually either saline or silicone gel. Because of this design, all breast implants can develop a tear or hole and leak their contents. Whether the hole or tear is large or small, it's called a rupture.

Ruptures can happen as implants age, or because of a blow to the chest, such as in a car accident or a bad fall. Tears or holes can be caused by a defective envelope, by a nick from a needle during a biopsy, or even when the surgeon is closing the incision in your chest after putting the implants inside you.

'The FDA found that most implant patients have at least one serious complication within three years after getting their silicone or saline implants.'

Things to consider before getting breast implants

The FDA (Food and Drug Administration) is responsible for protecting public health by assuring the safety, efficacy and security of medical devices. There are several important things to consider before deciding to undergo breast implant surgery, including understanding your own expectations and reasons for having the surgery. Below are some things the FDA thinks you should consider before undergoing breast augmentation, reconstruction or revision surgery.

Breast implants are not lifetime devices; the longer you have your implants, the more likely it will be for you to have them removed.

The longer you have breast implants, the more likely you are to experience local complications and adverse outcomes.

The most common local complications and adverse outcomes are capsular contracture, reoperation and implant removal. Other complications include rupture or deflation, wrinkling, asymmetry, scarring, pain, and infection at the incision site.

You should assume that you will need to have additional surgeries (reoperations).

Many of the changes to your breast following implantation may be cosmetically undesirable and irreversible.

If you have your implants removed but not replaced, you may experience changes to your natural breasts such as dimpling, puckering, wrinkling, breast tissue loss, or other undesirable cosmetic changes.

If you have breast implants, you will need to monitor your breasts for the rest of your life. If you notice any abnormal changes in your breasts, you will need to see a doctor promptly.

If you have silicone gel-filled breast implants, you will need to undergo periodic MRI examinations in order to detect ruptures that do not cause symptoms (silent ruptures). For early detection of silent rupture, the FDA recommends that women with silicone gel-filled breast implants receive MRI screenings 3 years after they receive a new implant and every 2 years after that. MRI screening for implant rupture is costly and may not be covered by your insurance.

Locating a plastic/cosmetic surgery specialist

If you have decided, after careful consideration and personal evaluation, that surgery is the option for you, then perhaps the most fundamentally important aspect of your experience is finding a reputable, qualified and skilled surgeon.

It is advised that you see more than one surgeon and have more than one consultation with each surgeon you talk to, also speak to other people who have had the same surgical procedure as you; experience and recommendations are highly valuable assets.

The Internet is also a valuable resource to those researching cosmetic surgery. Arming yourself with information and knowledge is the key to locating the right surgeon for you.

The British Association of Aesthetic Plastic Surgeons (BAAPS) has consumer safety guidelines in locating a surgeon. This highly valuable guide should be a reference point to those seeking a positive, safe experience with a reputable provider:

1. Make your own decisions – The real expert on your appearance and any concerns you may have is you. The only assistance you should need is to decide what, if any, surgery you might need; and you should ensure you get unbiased information regarding what might be technically possible and any associated risks and benefits. Do not let anyone talk you into doing anything for which you had little concern before the consultation.

2. Be informed – Anyone considering any cosmetic procedure should ensure they are fully informed and accept the limitations and risks of any procedure. Remember, no surgeon or procedure is 100% risk free.

3. Be comfortable – Make sure you feel comfortable with the organisation, surgeon and clinic you have chosen.

'Arming yourself with information and knowledge is the key to locating the right surgeon for you.'

4. Know your surgeon - Many practitioners purport to be experts, but many are not even surgeons. Practitioners may boast impressive sounding qualifications, but these can have little meaning. Organisations associated with and preferably based in the Royal College of Surgeons will demonstrate acceptable standards of practice, i.e. those which you can reasonably expect of surgeons and doctors in general. Hospitals which have strong associations with NHS consultants and practice will also adhere to these standards and so offer some level of reassurance. The BAAPS can help you find a properly credentialed surgeon in your area.

5. Get the timing right – Unless the circumstances are exceptional, avoid surgery if you have recently experienced major life events such as moving house, changing job, losing a loved one, the break-up of a relationship or the arrival of children.

'Unless the circumstances are exceptional, avoid surgery if you have recently experienced major life events.'

6. Beware of 'free' consultations and avoid booking fees or non-refundable deposits (a typical feature of many commercial clinics). Nothing is free, and if the surgery is right for you then there will be no need for you to be locked into going ahead by any financial cancellation penalties.

7. Think about location – Do not travel a long distance or overseas for any surgery unless you are comfortable with the arrangements to follow up and the management of any problems or complications which might arise.

8. Talk to Your GP – Your GP has no interest other than your welfare; so many doctors are very happy to advise patients and not be judgemental about something which many people feel very sensitive and vulnerable about.

9. You can always change your mind – Hopefully everything will be totally to your satisfaction, but remember you have the option to cancel right up until the time you go to sleep for surgery. The fundamental reason for the surgery is to make you feel better about yourself, and if this is compromised, surgery should not proceed. No reputable surgeon would normally impose any penalty for cancellations.

10. Take your time – Remember that undergoing surgery is a serious commitment.

You body, your choice

- If you decide to get breast implants put in or taken out, make sure you only use a specialist plastic surgeon.

- If your doctor shows photographs of patients, ask if they were his or her own patients. Ask to see photographs of how they looked a few years later.

- If your doctor tells you that breast implants are proven safe, ask for a copy of any report that studied women with implants for at least 10 years.

- Ask your doctor for written information about the risks of breast implants and read that information at least one week before surgery, so you have time to ask questions or gather more information.

- Any woman who considers silicone gel implants should ask for the informed consent form at least one week before surgery.

- If your doctor says all of his or her patients are happy with their results, ask to speak to patients who have had implants for at least 7-10 years.

Where should plastic surgery be carried out?

Safety first

All independent clinics and hospitals that provide cosmetic surgery must be licensed with the Care Quality Commission (CQC) to provide services.

This is to help ensure that patients are treated safely, and to reduce the risk of poor practice, anyone who provides any of the following cosmetic procedures must be registered with the Care Quality Commission by law:

- Any type of plastic surgery involving full or local anaesthetic.

- Treatments that use lasers, such as refractive eye surgery.

- Laser lipolysis (such as Smart Lipo).

The Care Quality Commission license and regulate cosmetic treatments that involve surgical procedures. They do not regulate the following services:

'All independent clinics and hospitals that provide cosmetic surgery must be licensed with the Care Quality Commission (CQC) to provide services.'

- Muscle-relaxing injections, for example Botox®.
- Remodelling techniques using cells, tissue or synthetic products (dermal fillers).
- Chemical peels.
- Non-surgical laser and intense light treatments (such as hair removal).

Things to consider before making a decision

Plastic or cosmetic surgery of any sort should not be undertaken lightly. It is important to remember that all surgery, including cosmetic procedures, involve risks. To minimise these risks, try to find out as much as you can about the provider and the procedure.

Find out about the provider

- First and foremost, choose your surgeon, doctor or practitioner on recommendation and do your research.
- Check that the hospital or clinic is registered with the Care Quality Commission, search for their details on the CQC website or ask them to show you their registration certificate. It is very important that you do not sign up for cosmetic surgery at a hospital or clinic that cannot show you that it is registered with the CQC.
- Remember, if the hospital or clinic is not registered with the CQC, their insurance may not cover them or you if anything goes wrong. This is because they are practising outside of the law.
- If you are considering plastic surgery, ask your GP to provide a referral to a surgeon. This will also ensure that your GP passes important information about your medical history to the surgeon.
- If you don't want to involve your GP, make sure that you choose a qualified and reputable surgeon that has been properly trained in the type of surgery you want. You should also check whether they are on the General Medical Council's specialist register. See the section locating a plastic/cosmetic surgery specialist.

- Make sure that the hospital or clinic will provide the care that you will need after the operation.

- Ask them to give you a copy of their patient's guide. This is a document that all cosmetic clinics and hospitals must provide. It gives details of all of the services they offer, the costs, and how patients can make comments and complaints.

- Be wary of 'special offers' which urge you to sign up to a procedure immediately. Cosmetic surgery is a serious decision which needs proper consideration – a good surgeon will want you to be absolutely sure about going ahead. If you feel that you are being placed under pressure to commit to anything before you are ready, walk away!

Making the decision

The decision to have plastic surgery should not be undertaken lightly. Plastic surgery can change your appearance in ways that you might consider desirable but it can be expensive in time and money and, although quite rare, it has been known to result in some changes to your appearance which you may not always find pleasing in the future. It is important that you do not feel pressurised or obliged to have it, nor is it wise to rush into making a choice without extensive research, it should be a decision you make only after a lot of careful thought and self-evaluation.

Being honest with yourself, and making a realistic evaluation about the way you feel and look is the most important part of making such an important and life-changing decision, and a decision over which you have control.

There are millions of people who have experienced the life-changing and positive influence that plastic surgery can bring to their lives, the chances for such successful outcomes really does begin with the right emotional and physiological foundation being firmly in place from the outset. If you are a physically and physcologically healthy adult, with the financial means to afford cosmetic surgery, then cosmetic surgery may be an option for you.

'There are millions of people who have experienced the life-changing and positive influence that plastic surgery can bring to their lives.'

Summing Up

※ There are 3 types of breast implant device, defined by their filler material: saline, silicone and composite.

※ It is impossible to predict how long an implant may last, some suffer problems after only a few weeks, whilst others last for many years.

※ The decision to undergo any form of breast surgery should not be undertaken lightly.

※ Carry out extensive research into the surgery, clinic and surgeon/doctor before agreeing to any procedure.

※ As with any surgical procedure, there are risks and potential complications involved in all forms of breast surgery, you should discuss these fully with your surgeon and doctor, so you fully understand them.

※ Ensure the hospital/clinic you choose is licensed with the Care Quality Commission.

※ Check the surgeon/doctor is registered on the General Medical Council's specialist register.

※ Beware of 'special offers' and any other attempts to pressure you into agreeing to a procedure.

Part 2

Poly Implant Prothèse (PIP Implants)

Chapter Eight

A Background and History of Poly Implant Prothèse (PIP)

Poly Implant Prothèse (PIP) was a French company started in 1991 that produced silicone gel breast implants. It was founded by a Frenchman called Jean-Claude Mas, born in 1939, a former medical sales representative. Poly Implant Prothèse went into liquidation in 2011. The company and its founder are at the heart of a public health-care scandal.

The company is said to have produced around 100,000 implants per year, during approximately 20 years. It is estimated that approximately 400,000 women worldwide may have PIP implant products implanted to enhance breast size or correct breasts for tissue loss.

PIP was once the world's third largest supplier of implants during their existence, PIP implants were supplied to women in 65 countries around the world who were thought to have had them fitted during surgery both for cosmetic reasons and in reconstructive surgery following treatment for breast cancer.

Breast implants were regulated under a European Union Medical Device Directive. PIP received a CE mark for their silicone gel breast implants in 2000 via the German Notified Body TÜV Rheinland, and started exports to the UK in that year. Between 2001 and 2009, about 80,000 implants (representing some 40,000 women) were sold in the UK.

'PIP was once the world's third largest supplier of implants during their existence.'

PIP implants were also exported to Latin American countries such as Brazil, Venezuela and Argentina; Western European markets including Britain, Germany, Spain and Italy, as well as Australia. PIP implants were never licensed for use in the United States.

PIP implants were also used in the UK under the name 'Rofil' and elsewhere in the world as 'M implants'.

It is estimated that between 2,000 and 3,000 of these implants were used by the National Health Service (NHS).

The majority of the remainder were used by the major Cosmetic Surgery Groups in the UK (including The Harley Medical Group, Transform and The Hospital Group) as well as other smaller providers and clinics.

It is believed that the implants were available to purchase for a mere £100 (up to £700 less than the medical-grade version), their low cost helped grow their popularity and helped PIP corner the market in cut-price prostheses.

'PIP implants were also used in the UK under the name "Rofil" and elsewhere in the world as "M implants".'

From about 2006 onwards, concerns began to emerge among cosmetic surgeons in the UK about the performance of PIP implants. The alarm was originally raised after many patients and surgeons reported premature rupturing.

Implants are designed to last a minimum of ten years, however the lifespan of PIP implants was averaging at as little as just three years.

In 2008, the UK based Medicines and Healthcare Products Regulatory Agency (MRHA) who enhance and safeguard the health of the public ensuring that medicines and medical devices work and are acceptably safe, noted an increase in the number of reports of ruptures being presented to them by patients and surgical professionals. This led the MHRA to raise concerns with the manufacturer – Poly Implant Prothèse – and the German Notified Body TÜV Rheinland. The MHRA raised further concerns in 2009.

After numerous complaints and concerns received, in March 2010 the French medical regulatory authority, Agence Francaise de Securite Sanitaire des Produits de Sante AFSSAPS, began an investigation into the company.

On the 29th March 2010, AFSSAPS informed the MHRA in the UK that it had suspended the marketing, distribution, export and the use of silicone gel-filled breast implants manufactured by Poly Implant Prothèse (PIP), they also recalled all of these devices in France.

Following an inspection of the PIP manufacturing plant, AFSSAPS established from their investigation that breast implants manufactured since 2001 had been fraudulently manufactured, using unsanctioned silicone gel: the breast implants that were being manufactured were being filled with a silicone gel containing a composition different from that which had been initially approved.

Poly Implant Prothèse had been using industrial grade silicone to fill breast implants instead of the medical grade specified for the CE mark. The low-grade industrial silicone was the type used to fill mattresses – and was never approved by health authorities. AFSSAPS revoked the CE mark.

MHRA promptly issued a medical device alert to all UK clinicians and cosmetic surgery providers, asking them to cease using the implants.

The Poly Implant Prothèse (PIP) factory was shut down and their products banned after it was found they had used the chemicals Baysilone, Silopren and Rhodorsil in their implants. These chemicals are normally used as a fuel additive or in the manufacture of industrial rubber tubing.

'Poly Implant Prothèse had been using industrial grade silicone to fill breast implants instead of the medical grade specified for the CE mark.'

Timeline

2001: PIP began to use unapproved in-house manufactured industrial-grade silicone instead of medical-grade silicone in the majority of its implants, although the French authorities have now said the use of defective PIP implants began earlier than 2001.

2003: The first signs of legal problems and financial losses can be traced by regulatory filings.

2009: Concerns surfaced in France first in 2009 when surgeons started reporting abnormally high rupture rates. This resulted in a flood of legal complaints and the company's bankruptcy

2010: TÜV Rheinland, headquartered in Germany, gave a quality certificate to the production process used by the company until March 2010. However, this didn't apply to the type of silicone used.

2010: In March 2010 PIP was placed into liquidation with losses of 9 million EUR after the French medical safety agency recalled its implants. In a subsequent inspection of the manufacturing site, the company was found to use unapproved industrial-grade silicone, with a cost of only 10% of an approved gel.

2011: On December 20th, French officials say that an action plan is underway following the death of a woman from ALCL (anaplastic large cell lymphoma). The French government recommended on December 23rd 2011, that 30,000 women in France seek removal of breast implants made of a suspect silicone gel by the worldwide exporting PIP firm.

Leaving aside the potential for the sale of some PIP implants prior to 2001, it is established that the non-approved silicone gel implants were manufactured and distributed principally between 2001 and 2009. These have the following model numbers:

- IMGHC-TX

- IMGHC-MX

- IMGHC-LS

'. . . all women with PIP implants should see a specialist.'

But note: There is suspicion that PIP and Rofil implants that were manufactured before 2001 are also affected and are prone to a higher rupture rate and therefore silicone leakage. Therefore, all women with PIP implants should see a specialist.

The issues surrounding PIP implants keep growing. Even though the FDA warned French authorities about the substandard quality of PIP implants in 2000, they continued to allow their use. The U.S Food and Drug Administration (FDA) sent PIP founder Jean-Claude Mas a strongly worded letter listing 11 'deviations' from 'good manufacturing practices', but that letter went ignored.

Psychological impact

A psychiatric study revealed that 80% of women affected by the recent Poly Implant Prothese (PIP) breast implant scandal will end up needing psychological counselling as a result of the stress caused.

The study, by the Clinical Partners and led by Richard Sherry, a counselling and clinical psychologist, discovered that nearly half (49%) had missed work due to stress about their potentially faulty implants. A further 40% admitted that their self-esteem had been 'severely' affected.

Over half (68%) confessed to feeling depressed after finding out about the breast implant scandal and a massive 92% admitted to suffering from stress-related insomnia since the news broke.

As a result of the upset caused, a third of women polled (33%) had sought help from a therapist or a doctor and 80% of them feel they will need psychological support in the future.

The participants of the study confessed to 'being in tears all the time' and being unable to think about anything but the 'alien' inside their body.

Richard Sherry stated that, 'Following a number of enquiries from women seeking support for the emotional issues they were facing following the PIP scare, I felt it was important to understand the greater impact this situation was creating for them and their families. Having a specialist interest in the psychology of cosmetic surgery, I knew that breasts in themselves can be complicated embodiments of femininity, sexuality and maternal identity. So when things go wrong – as they have rather catastrophically in this instance – it can trigger deep levels of anxiety and depression. The comments we received in this study really highlight the sever levels of distress being felt by those affected. It is important to foster communities of support.'

For more advice on emotional support relating to PIP implants please contact your GP who may be able to refer you for specialist support, or locate a reputable counsellor via the contacts listed in the help list.

You are not alone and there is help, your GP must understand your needs and act on them as professionally required to do so in accordance with Department of Health Guidelines.

Summing Up

- Poly Implant Prothèse (PIP) was a French company that produced and manufactured silicone gel breast implants between 2001 and 2010.

- From 2006 onwards, concerns emerged amongst surgical professionals about the performance of the PIP implants following reports of premature rupturing.

- In 2010, the French medical device regulatory authority (AFSSAPS) suspended the marketing, distribution, export and use of the implants manufactured by PIP, based on information gathered over the previous two years by the UK-based Medicines and Healthcare Products Regulatory Agency (MRHA).

- PIP officially went into liquidation in 2011, and is now at the centre of a health-care scandal after it was discovered Poly Implant Prothèse had been fraudulently manufacturing their implants. Instead of filling their products with a silicone gel containing the composition that had been initially approved and specified to carry the CE mark, they had been using low-grade industrial silicone that had never been approved by any medical authority.

- It is believed that some 40,000 women were given PIP implants in the UK, and following the investigation into PIP, anyone who has them is advised to speak to their doctor or the clinic the surgery was originally carried out.

Chapter Nine

Diagnosing Whether You Have PIP Implants

An estimated 40,000 PIP breast implants have been used for breast reconstruction and/or breast enlargements in the UK, in operations performed between 2001 and 2009. At the time of writing this book, news emerged in the UK of further cases of faulty implants having been inserted in women prior to 2001. In response to questions from the UK regulator, the Medicines and Healthcare products Regulatory Agency (MHRA), the French authorities have now said the use of defective PIP implants began earlier than 2001, potentially affecting 7,000 more women in Britain.

'Find out if you have PIP implants by checking your medical notes.'

Finding out if you have PIP implants

The government is advising women to take the following steps to reassure themselves if they have PIP implants, or if they need to find out if they have PIP implants:

▪ Find out if you have PIP implants by checking your medical notes. You can get this information for free from your clinic or through your GP. If you had PIP implants on the NHS, you should receive a letter, however if you do not receive one contact your GP.

▪ Speak to your clinic or cosmetic surgeon if you had them done privately; ask for information directly if you prefer. You can do this by requesting information from the supplier of the implants i.e. from the clinic which did the surgery or from the surgeon. Address the letter to the designated holder of the record. (This could be the clinic where the operation took place.) Include information so that they can identify your records – i.e. your name and address. (Further to this you may be sent an application form so you can access your records.) Specify exactly what you want to see. The person with this data must reply to your request within 40 days. They must reply within 21 days if the records have been added to in the last 40 days.)

If only requesting to view the records this could cost £10, as opposed to receiving copies which could cost up to £50. You will need to identify this when requesting. When viewing your records, you will need to look at the operation records page. This allows you to view stickers which will identify the makers of your implant. Those with PIP breast implants will see stickers reading 'PIP' or 'Cloverleaf Medical Implants'.

If a private clinic no longer exists, the government is advising women to speak to their GP.

'If a private clinic no longer exists, the government is advising women to speak to their GP.'

Once you have confirmed that your implants are PIP what to do next:

Scans

If you have PIP implants we would suggest that you contact your GP or the clinic where the operation took place to request a scan. This will enable the medical practitioner to assess whether your implants pose an immediate risk, i.e. if they are ruptured. You must be persistent in this if your request is denied.

The scan for breast implant review is either an ultrasound or an MRI. Ultrasound is reasonably available and cheap but it is not that accurate and depends on how experienced the person is who does it.

The MRI scan is more reliable but not as easily available and very expensive.

Since you often can't see a difference in your breast when a silicone gel implant breaks, it is important to have an MRI. A mammogram is not reliable enough for detecting a broken silicone gel implant, and the squeezing could make the contents of the implant leak outside the scar capsule.

MRI is the most sensitive imaging modality, as it is in most areas of diagnosis, but it also comes at a premium price. Good quality high resolution ultrasound is deemed by most doctors an accurate tool to detect implant rupture. The key in all of this though is the skill and experience of the reporting consultant radiologist.

When making an appointment to have your MRI scan you should check if the provider has a dedicated breast coil, as not all MRI providers have dedicated breast coils. Your MRI scan must also be provided by a specialist radiologist.

MRI providers will be able to provide you with detailed information regarding the scan and what the use of a breast coil involves.

It is important to note that you can currently take a request form for a diagnostic imaging service to any accredited diagnostic imaging provider. You may also wish to discuss your concerns with your specialist or GP at the time the diagnostic imaging request is made.

Once you have had the scan there are two outcomes:

* If your scan shows that your implants are ruptured and you would like them removed you would need to contact the clinic or surgeon to see what your options are.

* If your scan shows that there is currently no sign of any problems with the implant you will need to make the decision as to whether you would like them removed/replaced, or continue to monitor them.

Symptoms and signs of a ruptured breast implant

When a silicone gel breast implant breaks, the contents usually leak very slowly. A ruptured silicone gel implant can go completely unnoticed for many years. Sometimes the rupture is discovered only when the implant is removed.

A rupture is a split that occurs in the implant's casing. A rupture can be caused if:

* The implant's shell (that holds the silicone or saline) gets weaker over time.

'A ruptured silicone gel implant can go completely unnoticed for many years. Sometimes the rupture is discovered only when the implant is removed.'

- The implant is damaged during the operation.
- There is a flaw in the implant.
- The breast is injured.

When a silicone implant breaks, one of two things can happen to the leaking silicone gel. One possibility is that the leaking silicone can be contained within the scar tissue capsule, which is the thick layer of scar tissue that naturally builds up around the implant. When this happens, the silicone stays where it is. However, the silicone can leak outside of the scar tissue capsule. When this happens, silicone can migrate to other parts of the body, including the lymph nodes under the arm and major organs such as the lungs, where it is impossible to remove. The longer a woman waits to have a ruptured silicone gel implant removed, the more time the silicone has to travel in her body.

If your silicone gel implant ruptures, you could notice a change in the size or shape of your breast, pain or tenderness, swelling, numbness, burning or tingling. It is also highly possible to have a 'silent rupture', where you would not experience any of these symptoms. In this case, you would not know that your implant has broken.

Other symptoms include sudden swelling breasts; new discomfort; dragging pains; breast discomfort; warm, red, inflamed, tender to touch breasts, colour change; lumps around the implant; painful or non-tender lumps in the axilla; generally feeling unwell; and a broad spectrum of symptoms from 'not right' through to a tendency to be prone to infection, arthritis, dry eyes, general lethargy, renal and hepatic problems.

Other symptoms include a sensation of tingling under the nipple (followed by a complete loss of sensation, which over the years affects the entire breast), chronic back pain and 'pins and needles' down the arm on the side of the affected breast.

Many patients experience extreme fatigue, numbness and tingling, nausea, dizziness, heart palpitations, hair loss, depression, severe insomnia, ringing ears, weakness, stomach/headaches and anxiety.

Some patients experience discomfort in the armpit; also where an implant has ruptured the breast will lose the slight 'ridge' look that you get with implants; it may also feel a lot softer than the healthy breast, and look a lot 'flatter', which clearly signals a problem with the implant.

Do I need an MRI even if I just want them removed and replaced?

Scanning by ultrasound or MRI may be useful in helping to confirm whether or not the implant has ruptured. However, if a patient has already decided (after clinical advice) to have the implant removed, scanning is usually unnecessary.

Summing Up

* To find out if you have PIP implants, the government advises checking your original medical notes. This can be done by either obtaining them from the clinic or your GP. If the procedure was performed at a private clinic you can send a written request direct to the clinic or surgeon for the information.

* If it is confirmed you have PIP implants, you should contact your GP or the clinic the surgery took place. An MRI scan can determine the condition of the implants.

* There are many signs and symptoms associated with a ruptured breast implant, so it is important you are aware of them and can recognise them so you can seek medical help if necessary.

Chapter Ten

Your Choices

Following the investigation into PIP, which resulted in the current health-care scandal affecting thousands of women in the UK, the Health Secretary, Andrew Lansley, announced the NHS would perform free PIP implant removal operations. This offer was also extended to patients who were given PIP implants from a private clinic and were unable to access their original provider for removal treatment. However, free replacement operations would only be considered for patients who had originally received PIP implants from the NHS, and therefore anyone who was treated at a private clinic originally would not be eligible for replacement treatment, unless it was deemed clinically necessary.

What to do if you received PIP implants on the NHS

All women who have received a PIP implant from the NHS will be contacted in due course to inform them that they have a PIP implant and to provide relevant information and advice. If, in the meantime, NHS patients seek information about the make of their implant then this will be provided free of charge.

- Women who wish to will be able to seek a consultation with their GP, or with the surgical team who carried out the original implant, to seek clinical advice on the best way forward.

- If the woman chooses, this could include a non-urgent examination by imaging to see if there is any evidence that the implant has ruptured.

- The NHS will support removal of PIP implants if, informed by an assessment of clinical need, risk or the impact of unresolved concerns, a woman with her doctor decides that it is right to do so. The NHS will replace the implants if the original operation was done by the NHS.

GP referrals to specialist services

If, on clinical examination, a GP finds symptoms which suggest the possibility of new breast disease, they will refer the patient urgently to a rapid access breast service, even if the original implant was from a private provider. Other referrals should be made to the regional breast reconstructive service or local equivalent (for patients who received implants as part of NHS treatment) or to the original clinic (for implants provided privately) and are unlikely to need fast-track referral.

'Not every single PIP implant will need to come out, especially if it hasn't ruptured, but if you do want to get your implants removed, the NHS has a duty to remove your implants for you.'

What NHS choices you have if you had your breast implants in the private sector

If you have been treated in the private sector but can no longer trace your surgeon, the NHS has agreed to treat you. You need to contact your GP first who should then refer you to a local NHS clinic. The GP must give advice to you as part of the directive from the Department of Health.

Not every single PIP implant will need to come out, especially if it hasn't ruptured, but if you do want to get your implants removed, the NHS has a duty to remove your implants for you.

If you contact your GP and state that you originally received an implant from a private provider, your GP will encourage you to go back to the original provider for advice, scanning if appropriate, and removal or replacement of the implant if desired.

However, if the original provider has gone out of business, or is unwilling to help, your GP should carry out a clinical examination and refer onwards to specialist NHS services as indicated above. At this stage your GP will make it clear that the NHS is not offering to pay for a replacement implant.

If you had your PIP implants in the private sector

All women who have received a PIP implant from the private sector such as a private surgeon, clinic, or surgery provider are urged by the Department of Health to seek a consultation with their GP.

Your GP will probably advise you to contact the original provider. Women should be able contact the surgical team who carried out the original implant; it is the original provider's duty to give a patient clinical advice on the best way forward.

To obtain a copy of your medical records, please write to your originating clinic. On receipt of a signed written request the clinic will arrange to send you a copy of your medical records. You may be asked to be patient as some large surgery providers have been inundated with requests to access thousands of patient medical records. Your records will indicate your date and time of surgery including confirmation that PIP implants were used.

In accordance with The Data Protection Act 1998, which prohibits the retention of personal data for longer than is necessary, some clinics destroy patient records after a period of 8 years, meaning that there is the potential that records no longer exist.

If your original surgery took place over eight years ago, but your private surgical provider cannot find your records you are advised to consult with your GP who may be able to trace any information through your medical records, but if this is not successful your GP should advise on the best course of action in your individual circumstances.

'Most private cosmetic surgery providers are now offering free consultation and removal for women who received PIP implants as former clients from 2001.'

Most private cosmetic surgery providers are now offering free consultation and removal for women who received PIP implants as former clients from 2001 – but most large commercial surgical providers, such as The Harley Medical Group, Transform and The Hospital Group, will not give free replacement implants to women. If you want replacement breast implants as a private cosmetic surgery patient, you will be asked to pay for them as part of a surgical procedure.

Essentially, large commercial private surgical providers have agreed to match the NHS offer made by Andrew Lansley, the Health Secretary, which was to agree to allow access to women who wanted their PIP implant removal operations performed for free on the NHS. However, Mr Lansley refused to extend that to cover free replacements, unless women received PIPs on the NHS.

If you are a patient that has had PIP implants with a private surgical provider here are some tips for dealing with your consultations:

Tips by an expert surgeon

Mr Jonathan Staiano has over 10 years' experience in plastic surgery and has a dedicated practice specialising in cosmetic and reconstructive breast surgery. He is a full member of BAAPS and BAPRAS.

Mr Staiano treats patients with all forms of breast asymmetry, including tuberous breast deformity, and chest wall deformity as well as regularly performing breast enlargement, reduction and uplift surgery.

His tips for a consultation when seeking cosmetic surgery privately are:

- Is your surgeon a plastic surgeon?

- Is your surgeon a 'breast' specialist?

- Ask the surgeon – what if I have a complication as a result of my surgery, will I have to pay for additional surgery?

- Does the price of my surgery include follow-up care such as post-operative appointments?

- When will my post-operative appointments be? (Ask your surgeon to give you a timeline) For example will post-operative appointments be at 1 week? 1 month? 1 year? 5 years? (Ask: will I have to pay for these?)

- Ask your surgeon where your operation will be performed – try to make sure you stay close to home as this makes post-operative appointments easier for you.

- Ask which implants your surgeon has selected for your surgery, and ask him to explain his choices, ask what warranty the implants have, do your research on the selected implants.

- Ask your surgeon what alternatives there may be in your individual case, he may suggest alternatives such as 'fat grafting' if you are welcome to understanding the choices.

Patients who have had their breast augmentation with PIP implants in the private sector and have no symptoms

You should contact your private provider and ask for a consultation. The government and all the surgical associations expect the private providers who used PIP implants to take the responsibility of duty of care towards their patients seriously and treat them with dignity and compassion.

The Department of Health has issued guidelines to GPs stating that patients should not be referred for scanning (USS/MRI) before receiving a specialist surgical opinion.

The Department of Health guidelines state that; for matters relating to patients without signs or symptoms of rupture, scanning should only be used to assist decision-making where the patient is uncertain of whether to have the implant removed or where rupture is identified. For all patients who have already decided to undergo removal of PIP implants scanning is unnecessary.

Summing Up

■ Women who received PIP implants from the NHS will be contacted to inform them of this, and of the choices they now face.

■ The NHS has agreed to provide free removal treatment to its original patients.

■ Women who received PIP implants from a private surgeon, clinic or surgery provider should consult with their GP who will then offer advice on their next course of action. If they haven't already done so, their GP will advise them to contact their original provider of the implants, as it is the provider's duty to advise on the best way forward.

■ If you are a private patient whose original provider has since gone out of business or is refusing to help, your GP should carry out a clinical examination and then refer you onwards to a specialist in the NHS. The NHS has agreed to treat patients in these circumstances, but will only perform free removal procedures, they will not replace the implants unless clinically necessary.

Chapter Eleven

Surgical Removal
of Implants

Removal of an intact implant

Removal of an intact implant is generally not recommended due to the risks involved in having surgery, such as infection, bleeding and reaction to the anaesthesia. However, women whose implants are intact but who are ill from other complications sometimes find that their health improves dramatically after removal. A study of removed implants that were not replaced, carried out by Noreen Aziz and her colleagues, found that 97% of women with pain and other rheumatology symptoms felt better after their implants were removed and not replaced. Many symptoms lessened or disappeared over the next few months. In contrast, 96% of the women who did not have their implants removed became even more ill.

Removing intact implants is not always complicated, but it can be very difficult to remove certain kinds of implants, such as foam-covered implants (polyurethane), implants with hard capsules surrounding them, and implants that have ruptured. This kind of explanation sometimes involves removal of not just the implants, but also removal of some of the tissue and muscle surrounding the implant.

Removal of a silicone gel implant is more complicated than having it put in. This is particularly true if the implant is leaking or has ruptured, because it's very important to ensure that silicone gel from a broken implant does not spill or remain in the body.

'Removal of an intact implant is generally not recommended due to the risks involved in having surgery.'

The surgeon who performed the original surgery is not necessarily the best choice for removing the implants. Explantation (removal of a breast implant) results can be excellent or disastrous. Some plastic or cosmetic surgeons are very experienced at implantation, but not explantation. However, there are some plastic surgeons who are very experienced at removal and are especially skilled at getting the best possible cosmetic result. The surgeon you choose should be experienced with explantation, specialist registered as a plastic surgeon, and should be willing to show you pictures of many patients with post-explantation results, or better still, offer to have former patients talk to you. Find out if they were happy with their doctor and with their results.

Removal of implants en bloc

'Removing implants en bloc is particularly recommended by experts if you have become sick since receiving your implants.'

Most experts believe that removing the implants 'en bloc' is very important. This means that the entire implant and the entire scar tissue capsule surrounding it are all removed together. Although it is more difficult than removing just the implants, it makes it easier to remove any silicone that may have leaked from a broken gel implant, and also helps remove silicone or other chemicals that may have bled from the silicone outer envelope. You should ask your surgeon if he/she would use this procedure.

Removing implants en bloc is particularly recommended by experts if you have become sick since receiving your implants. Some experts believe that symptoms such as joint pains, chronic flu-like symptoms, memory loss, confusion, or a burning sensation could be a result of silicone that has leaked from your implant, and perhaps outside the scar tissue capsule. If this is the case, leaving the scar tissue capsules, or part of them, and/or silicone in your body, probably isn't going to let you recover as well as you might. It is also possible that while the silicone did not make you sick before, silicone that is left behind after explantation could make you sick later, because your body will respond to this foreign material.

Some surgeons discourage patients from removing their implants without replacing them, because they believe implants are safe and because they're concerned that the patient will be very unhappy with her appearance after the implant is removed. The breast tissue stretches from the implant, and if the surgeon isn't skilled in explantation without replacement, the breast is unlikely to be as attractive as it was before the implant surgery. If the surgeon is not

80

skilled at removing ruptured implants, the silicone can spill into healthy breast tissue, which then may need to be removed as part of the surgery. However, after an experienced explant surgeon removes implants, many women are very pleased with the way their breasts look and feel.

An expert's point of view

Ruth Waters, Consultant Plastic Surgeon at Queen Elizabeth Hospital, Birmingham, gives her view on PIP implants:

'If I had a PIP implants, I would want them removed even if there wasn't a rupture because they are not a good quality implant and the shell of the implant is not strong so it could lead to problems in the future. There is no risk to a patient's general health if there is a small leak of silicone. However, if it is left for a long period, the surgery can get more complicated to do.'

What happens to the faulty implants that are removed from patients?

A ruptured implant should be discarded unless arrangements for examination have been made with the Medicines and Healthcare products Regulatory Agency.

Surgeons are encouraged by the Chief Medical Officer, Professor Dame Sally C Davies, to collect all available data at the time of consultation and surgery. This data collection is then made available to many relevant surgical organisations.

Ongoing review of clinical guidance

The Association of Breast Surgery, the British Association of Plastic and Reconstructive Aesthetic Surgeons, the British Association of Aesthetic Plastic Surgeons, the Federation of Surgical Speciality Associations and the Royal College of Surgeons all participated in an expert group convened by Professor

Sir Bruce Keogh to review policy in relation to breast implants from the French company Poly Implant Prothèse (PIP). All organisations have endorsed the findings of the interim report published on 6th January 2012.

These five professional surgical organisations are now independently publishing further clinical guidance for GPs and surgeons regarding the care of patients who have received PIP breast implants.

This means that the government and these various associations are working hard to ensure that you are constantly kept up to date through the advice and care that your GP, surgeons and surgical providers give you.

It is expected that all GPs, surgeons and surgical providers will offer advice and care based on these guidelines, together with a compassionate and caring attitude for all patients.

The Department of Health has urged all surgeons and surgical providers responsible for breast augmentations using PIP implants to undertake replacement surgery without making a charge to the patients. However this is at the discretion of a surgeon or a surgical provider.

Surgeons and hospital specialists reviewing patients with PIP implants should carefully assess the patient for the possibility of rupture or leak. Those patients who have evidence of implant rupture should be advised regarding the implications of implant removal and replacement. They should also be advised of the risk benefit ratio in respect of removal and replacement.

If the surgery was carried out by the NHS patients will be offered re-implantation.

'The Department of Health has urged all surgeons and surgical providers responsible for breast augmentations using PIP implants to undertake replacement surgery without making a charge to the patients.'

Future monitoring

Patients who have undergone surgery to remove their PIP implants following a rupture or a gel leak should be advised to attend annual follow-up consultations for at least two years.

Patients who underwent a 'clean' explantation or re-implantation should be advised about normal follow-up procedures.

Where a patient decides, after consultation with specialist, not to have their PIP implants removed, they should be followed up on an annual basis. In the case of NHS patients this review would normally be carried out by the GP; private patients should be followed up by the surgeon or provider responsible for the original implantation. Patients with PIP implants should be made aware of the signs and symptoms of implant rupture and gel bleed.

Have I considered all the options?

Cosmetic surgery is not the only option available to you, this is something that the cosmetic surgeons you consult with will point out to you, you may also find that cosmetic surgeons you talk to will suggest alternative and different ways to address your concerns. Knowing and understanding all of your options gives you a better chance of making a decision you are happy with. Don't be afraid to have second consultations with surgeons to clarify the advice you have been given, and use your time effectively to find out about alternative solutions and treatments suggested to you before making that final decision.

For patients from the private sector who have been unable to secure help from their original provider, the NHS will offer implant removal, but no re-implantation will be offered. Implant replacements as a private patient will have to be paid for.

Where a patient decides, after consultation with her GP or specialist, not to have an explanation, she should be followed up on an annual basis. This review would normally be carried out by the GP (for NHS patients) or by the clinic which carried out the original implant (for private patients).

'Knowing and understanding all of your options gives you a better chance of making a decision you are happy with.'

Summing Up

- If implants are intact, i.e. not leaking or ruptured, it is generally not recommended they are removed, due to the risks involved in surgery.

- Removal of a silicone implant is more complicated than having it put in.

- It is not necessarily the best choice to have the surgeon who put the implants in remove them. Some surgeons are more skilled and experienced in implant removal than others.

- Since the findings of the investigation into PIP, several organisations, including The Association of Breast Surgery and the Royal College of Surgeons, are publishing clinical guidelines for GPs and surgeons to follow regarding the advice and care given to patients who received PIP implants.

Chapter Twelve

Costs and Legal Support

How much does it cost to replace a bad PIP implant?

If you are seeking the removal and replacement of PIP implants on a private basis there are costs and considerations to think about before you commit to surgery.

Many cosmetic surgery clinics, providers and surgeons are offering reduced rates and fees to patients with PIP implants in order to allow them affordable access to their services. Prices tend to start at £2,000 to £3,500, some are charging higher prices for removal and replacement surgery of PIP implants. It does vary depending on the surgeon or clinical provider involved, and the location.

Many private surgical providers such as Transform, The Harley Medical Group and The Hospital Group are offering free removal of implants to patients, but charging fees to replace with new implants. The current general fee scale with large surgical providers ranges from approximately £1,500 to £2,500 onwards.

It is estimated that 95% of the 40,000 women in the UK with PIP implants had them fitted at a private clinic.

The following clinics have stated that they will replace the PIP implants at no cost to the patient where it is deemed clinically necessary:

- Holly House.
- Highgate Hospitals.
- Make Yourself Amazing.
- Ramsay Health Care

'It is estimated that 95% of the 40,000 women in the UK with PIP implants had them fitted at a private clinic.'

- BMI Healthcare.
- Nuffield Healthcare.
- HCA International.
- Spire Healthcare.

Patients who have had PIP implants placed by the NHS

As discussed in chapter 10, all women who have received a PIP implant from the NHS will be contacted to inform them that they have a PIP implant and to provide relevant information and advice. These patients will be offered surgery for the removal or the removal and replacement of PIP implants at no cost.

Patients who had PIP implants through a private clinic which no longer exists

If you were a patient of a private clinic which no longer exists, or the clinic where you had the procedure is refusing to help, the Department of Health has confirmed that the NHS will take out ruptured implants at no cost to the patient. You should contact your GP to discuss this option. The NHS will remove private clinic implants but will only replace them where it is clinically necessary. The NHS will not replace your PIP implants with new implants (see chapter 10 for more information). However some limited NHS hospitals are offering 'top up' schemes to patients who are not eligible for replacement implants at NHS expense and who offer to pay for replacements as a private transaction. General guidance on this kind of 'top up' scheme can be obtained by visiting the Department of Health website as this is currently only available in very limited hospitals in the UK. In this case the patient elects to pay for the additional costs of a replacement as part of a single operation in which the NHS pays for the costs of removal. Plastic surgery isn't widely available on the NHS. It isn't available for cosmetic purposes – for example, if you feel you'd look better with slimmer thighs or a smaller nose.

As everyone knows, the NHS only has a limited amount of money and this needs to be spent carefully so other patients who need treatment don't lose out.

The official NHS website may be a good resource to contact if you are researching NHS top-up schemes. (See the help list.)

Have you factored the cost of surgery into your overall decision?

If you have saved the money for your procedure and you have made the choice to have surgery to feel better in your health and wellbeing, then that is good.

However if you do not have the funds readily available for your procedure then you may want to consider several options as to how to fund your surgery so you can move forward with your plans.

Many cosmetic surgery clinics and surgeons now offer flexible finance options and plans whereby you can pay for your surgery on a monthly credit basis, alternatively banks and building societies now offer loans for people considering cosmetic surgery.

It is advisable not to put yourself under financial stress if you do not have the means to pay for your surgery as this could affect your credit rating and harm your financial status in the future. Having to worry in addition to your recovery and healing about the financial stress you have put yourself under to cover the cost of your surgery is not the best situation to be in. The best solution may be to plan, and save and wait until you are in a position where you can comfortably afford the surgical procedures without placing yourself under any unnecessary stress or liability.

Legal support

Most people have cosmetic surgery to improve their appearance and increase their self-confidence, so it can be all the more devastating to spend valuable saving and finances on surgery, only to be left with an adverse situation.

If you are looking to take legal advice regarding your individual situation with PIP implants, it is ideal to source a law company that will deal sensitively and professionally with your cosmetic surgery claim. It is also a benefit to your circumstances to source a law company that have expert medical negligence solicitors.

Grounds for pursuing a claim

Many women are contacting specialist law companies to pursue claims against PIP breast implant surgical providers. Most of the claims presented to law companies by PIP victims are based on allegations that the providers of the surgery have breached the contract that exists between the provider and patient.

'If you are looking to take legal advice regarding PIP implants, it is ideal to source a law company that have expert medical negligence solicitors.'

Certainly where the PIP implant is proven to be a 'defective product' and not of satisfactory quality, a breach of contract can be argued under the Sale of Goods Act 1979 and Supply of Goods and Services Act 1982.

If a breach of contract is proven then the remedy is given in the form of damages which are then used to put the patient in the position that they would have been in had the clinic/surgeon not breached their contract and had they not been sold defective implants. Despite the fact that the goods are now inside your body and surgery is needed to replace them, this does not leave the law ineffective and the same rules apply. Any expenses incurred and damages for the further surgery and effects of the medical issues caused by this scandal may also see compensation for personal injuries being paid to the victims.

Many PIP implant victims have found themselves in circumstances where they have experienced injuries or illness as a result of the defective PIP implants. Some victims are also claiming that these have been significant enough to cause a 'loss'. The losses that PIP victims are claiming stem from the breach of contract that arose between themselves as a patient and the surgical provider. As a result of this many women are now pursuing a personal injury compensation claim.

There are other issues and complexities regarding PIP claims, but the 'breach of provider and patient contract' principle is the basic foundation of most claims.

If, in some cases, where judgement cannot be successfully attained, then consideration will be be given to the way in which the implants were paid for. If the implants were paid for in full or part by a credit card or by finance, then it may be possible for a claim to be brought against the credit provider under the Consumer Credit Act 1974.

Summing Up

- It is estimated that of the 40,000 women in the UK with PIP implants, 95% of them were fitted in private clinics.

- Many private surgeons and clinics are offering reduced rates and fees to patients with PIP implants. Prices offered vary from provider to provider and are dependent upon an number of factors, such as location.

- Patients who had PIP implants fitted from the NHS will be offered removal and/or removal and replacement procedures free of charge.

- The NHS will remove ruptured implants at no cost to patients who originally had them put in by a private clinic that either no longer exists or is unwilling to help. However, the NHS will only provide replacement surgery when it is clinically necessary, otherwise the patient must finance the replacement surgery themselves or look into the NHS' 'top-up' scheme.

- Patients looking to pursue legal action regarding their situation with PIP implants should seek advice from a law company with expert medical negligence solicitors.

Chapter Thirteen

FAQs

Stories about breast implants are always topical and of interest but sometimes the reporting can create alarm without reason. Here are some frequently asked questions and answers relating to PIP implants.

In the UK the competent authority is the MHRA (Medicines and Healthcare products Regulatory Agency) who have been monitoring many different aspects for PIP breast implant safety since the French regulators identified a problem with manufacturing standards nearly a year ago. The MHRA has commissioned detailed and searching tests in all aspects of safety for these implants. Like those conducted in France and other countries, they have so far shown no cause for alarm or any indication that these implants pose a risk to health.

Are PIP implants toxic?

Tests that have taken place on the silicone gel filler material used in the PIP breast implants do not currently show any genotoxic effects for the PIP silicone gel filler material. There is no reason to suspect they can cause breast cancer, nor is there any evidence of health risks, whether they are ruptured or not.

Advice to patients from the Medicines and Healthcare products Regulatory Agency (MHRA), the UK government agency which is responsible for ensuring that medicines and medical devices work effectively and are safe, continues to be that there is no evidence of any abnormal health effects associated with the implant filler material. For further information visit: www.mhra.gov.uk/

The MHRA is working closely with the French Authorities (the AFSSAPS www.afssaps.fr/) and reviewing all information available.

Should I have my implants removed anyway?

All breast implants have a limited life. The normal recommendation is that for women whose breasts remain free of any new symptoms (as most breasts with implants do) then at ten years after implantation it is wise to have them checked by a surgeon. In most cases no action other than monitoring over the years is needed.

It is thought that the manufacturing standards of PIP implants may make them prone to need removal or exchange earlier than most. Women concerned should consult their implanting surgeon or a surgeon experienced in breast augmentation.

My GP will not arrange a scan, what should I do?

If you have clinical symptoms and your GP will not arrange a scan, you will have to obtain one privately, unless there is a clinical need for your GP to refer you.

What are the current NHS recommendations?

The latest advice from the NHS and plastic surgery experts is that women with PIP breast implants do not need to have them removed unless they have symptoms such as pain and tenderness.

There is no link to cancer and there is no clear evidence of an increased risk of harm compared to other brands of breast implants.

However, if you are concerned, you should find out if you have PIP implants by checking your medical notes. You can get this information from your clinic or through your GP. If you had PIP implants on the NHS, you will receive a letter.

Speak to your specialist or GP if you had them done on the NHS, or your clinic if you had them done privately.

Agree what's best for you. Get advice on whether or not you need a scan, and then discuss appropriate action with your doctor.

How will I deal with any surgical complications?

All surgery, no matter what kind, carries risks and complications. If you unfortunately happen to be one of the patients who experience a rare serious complication as a result of your surgery, you must be prepared to deal with it from the outset of your decision-making. It is essential that you accept that complications can happen. However if you feel that you are not physically or emotionally equipped to deal with a possible complication, which could be anything such as delayed healing time, or additional surgery, or side effects; then simply don't do it. It is impossible to predict if complications will occur from any type of surgery as each individual patient responds to recovery and healing in a very unique and different way.

What can you do to protect yourself if you have private surgery?

In the first place talk to your GP, who can recommend surgeons and advise you about any personal health issues you will need to raise with the surgeon.

All companies that provide cosmetic surgery in the UK must be registered with the Healthcare Commission. Ask to see their annual registration details and don't book surgery with companies that can't provide this information.

When you approach different companies about cosmetic surgery, you will have an initial appointment to discuss your needs.

The Department of Health recommends this first appointment should only be with a person who is medically qualified – that means a doctor or nurse. Again, you can check their registration number with the councils that regulate them.

Your next appointment should be with the surgeon who is going to perform the operation. Make sure the procedure is fully explained to you and that you understand what is going to happen in terms of surgery, risks, scars and recovery time.

Ask about the surgeon's qualifications and write them down so you can check them with the relevant organisations later. Ask how many times they've performed the operation and how many patients needed corrective surgery.

The surgeon should give you information to take away. Don't be afraid to get a second opinion or to approach a different company if you have any concerns.

You should only book surgery once you've had time to think things through and you shouldn't feel pressured to confirm anything on the day.

Make sure you get a written statement about costs and understand what's included in the price and when you need to pay.

The following FAQs have been answered by various law companies.

Can I get my PIP implants replaced now, or do I have to wait for the outcome of my claim?

It is of course your choice as to what course of action you take, but a sensible legal view is that obviously your health should come first. There is no legal reason to delay the removal/replacement of your PIP implants. If you are going to have them removed, however, it is suggested that if you are considering legal action you take certain precautionary measures. It is advisable that you get photographic evidence of your PIP implants before and after the further treatment, try and get a medical report following surgery detailing the state your implants were found in, and keep all evidence of your financial, physical, and psychological losses. If you are going to have surgery then your solicitors know this so they can make sure your file is up to date.

I have had PIP implants in the last 10 years. What should I do?

If you have any medical symptoms you should see your GP. If your original treatment was on the NHS you may be referred for an ultrasound scan to check for any damage to the implants, and/or to a consultant. If you have the need for further surgery this should be done free by the NHS. If your operation was performed privately you should go back to the clinic. They may charge you for any further treatment including a scan, or suggest you go to see your GP to get the scan done. Some GPs appear reluctant to refer patients who had private surgery for an NHS scan. If the clinic refuses to carry out a scan go back to your GP for advice.

I cannot afford to pay privately for replacement surgery and the NHS

will not replace my PIP implants – what can I do?

If the clinic/s are denying liability and refusing to fund your treatment then that is something that a solicitor is going to have to argue for as a part of your claim, and this can take time.

If you find yourself in this difficult position, it is suggested that you try and obtain a scan and notify your solicitor and your GP of the outcome. Your GP can advise you on where you stand medically and your solicitors can formally notify the defendant of the details of your particular case in what is called a letter of claim. Within this your solicitor can make it clear that they would be looking for them to fund the treatment you need.

My privately funded implant has ruptured and the clinic says I must pay for removal and/or replacement. Can they do this?

Just as if you had purchased any other goods or service, if it is defective you are entitled to be compensated. However, just like any other business, the clinic may not agree. If they refuse, you need to seek urgent legal advice. If you decide to pay then keep details so you can claim the costs back later. If the implants have not yet ruptured, a solicitor may think that the increased risk of rupture still makes them 'defective', this needs consideration from your solicitor.

I paid for the surgery on a credit card. Does this make a difference?

Under the Consumer Credit Act the credit provider may well be liable to compensate you for the cost of further surgery and any injury caused, though they may want you to pursue the clinic too.

The private clinic has disappeared. Can I still make a claim?

All clinics should have been insured and your solicitor should be able to advise you if and how they may able to identify those insurers.

My symptoms are similar to what other women complain of – pain, inflammation and/or tiredness. Is there any evidence linking these symptoms to the implants?

The UK government's medical advisors do not presently believe there is a link, but the French advisors apparently think the risk of problems, even where the implants have not ruptured, justifies removal. This is confusing. Your doctor will know the latest advice when it is given by the government.

What if I have my PIP implants replaced and paid for privately – can I still claim compensation?

Keep your receipts and details of travelling expenses, loss of earnings (try and take unpaid leave or get yourself signed off work rather than take it as holiday), childcare fees, parking, reasonable accommodation fees and so forth. If you can prove you have reasonably incurred such losses, your solicitor may be able to factor those into your claim for PIP compensation.

Similarly, if you have your PIP implants removed or replaced on the NHS free of charge, you could still bring a claim for compensation. This is because the compensation that would be sought for you does not only comprise of financial loss – it also takes into account any physical and/or psychological loss you have undergone due to the PIP implants.

What happens if I decide to get the implants removed and they are not ruptured?

A woman who is worried and decides to pay for removal even if they are not yet ruptured may be able to reclaim such costs, but will probably require legal advice and assistance to do so.

My implants ruptured within the last 3 years and I have suffered trauma, out-of-pocket expenses and loss of income. Can I claim?

A solicitor dealing with medical negligence will be able to assess your individual circumstances and evaluate whether a claim can be presented. It is advisable to produce as much information and evidence as possible to support your claim.

In summary

At the present time, many legal claims against surgical providers are still in their early stages and very much in infancy of any concrete legal development.

If you are a woman with PIP breast implants and you have legal concerns you should, in the first instance, seek advice in a medical context from your surgeon or GP, to agree on an appropriate course of action. Your health and wellbeing is the overall priority in this and thereafter. For those who wish to make a claim for compensation, independent legal advice should be sought.

An Expert's View

By Mr Adrian Richards MBBS MSc FRCS (Plast.) of Aurora Clinics

Aurora Clinics never used PIP implants, but have been helping many of the unfortunate 30,000-40,000 reported women in the UK who have these fragile and potentially unsafe implants. Aurora have also produced advice guides for patients, surgeons and GPs to help them understand the complexities of dealing with PIPs. Here are some key observations and recommendations that Aurora Clinics have been making:

Recurring problems with PIP implants

The recurrent problems that our surgeons witness when removing PIP implants are with the implant shell and the implant contents.

The shell of every silicone implant is made through a separate dipping and drying process. In PIPs, it appears that the numbers of dips was reduced; in particular the most expensive layer, which seals the shell from the internal silicone, may have been omitted entirely. This means that the implant is permeable to the internal silicone, resulting in 'bleed' of the internal silicone through the shell. This is by far the most common PIP problem that we are noting when women come for removal and in some cases it is so severe that, whilst the shell itself is still intact, virtually the entire content has bled out.

This content is acknowledged to be industrial grade silicone, which is less expensive and has not been tested on humans. Medical grade silicone is expensive and has been tested internally on humans. It appears that, to reduce costs, a mixture of both types of silicone was used in PIP implants. Ongoing toxicology studies are being performed on this silicone but we do not have any definitive data on this at present.

In addition, the actual shell of PIP implants appears to be more fragile than other implant brands, with a higher rupture rate.

Findings

One of the reasons why definitive data is lacking on PIP issues is that there is no national registry of these implants. A registry did exist but the government withdrew funding for this in the mid 2000s.

Because of this, we do not know exactly how many PIP implants were used in the UK or which women have them. The government is now calling for the breast implant registry to be re-established.

Aurora Clinic's surgeons are working with major professional bodies, BAAPS and BAPRAS, to record data on the PIP implants we remove.

Our findings to date indicate that of the PIP implants we have removed:

- 25% are severely ruptured.

- 70% have significant silicone gel-bleed on their surfaces.

- 5% are in a similar condition to other implant brands when removed.

We acknowledge that this is a slightly skewed result as the people I am seeing are more likely to have problems with their implants as they are having surgery. However, it is showing that the vast majority have a gel-bleed or rupture. Further analysis of the performance of particular batches of PIP implants is ongoing. Many of the implants that have ruptured have only been inserted within the last 4 years.

Recommendations

Because of these findings, we feel that all women with PIP implants should consider having them removed.

If women with PIP implants do not have information on their implant manufacturer they should request this from the surgeon or company who inserted them. This should be provided promptly and efficiently.

The requested information should include the:

- Size in CCs.

- Type (high, ultrahigh (UH) etc.)

- The batch and lot number. The batch number is a 5 digit number and the lot number a 3 digit number.

Glossary

Anaesthesia

Loss of feeling or awareness that is induced and monitored during a surgical procedure. General anaesthesia, which produces an unconscious state, is commonly used during breast augmentation surgery.

Anatomical

Refers to shaped or contoured breast implants that are designed to give the breasts a natural shape.

Areola

The area of darker tissue that surrounds the nipple and which contain the Montgomery's glands.

Armpit incision

An incision used in breast augmentation surgery made in the armpit. Also called the transaxillary incision.

Asymmetry

Refers to a woman's breasts that differ in size, shape and/or position. Most women actually have some degree of asymmetry, but significant asymmetry after breast augmentation may require an adjustment procedure.

Augmentation mammoplasty

A procedure to reshape and enlarge the breast for cosmetic reasons or to reconstruct the breast.

Band size

A measurement is taken around the body, underneath the breasts to determine the band length of a bra. Expressed as a number that precedes the cup size to indicate the overall bra size, e.g. 42C.

Bilateral

Pertains to corresponding parts on both sides of the body, such as referring to both the left and right breasts.

Biopsy

Removal of sample tissue to test for cancer, including breast cancer.

Bottoming out

Occurs when the breast implant is positioned too low on the chest and the nipple rides too high, resulting in an unnatural look.

Breast augmentation

A surgical procedure designed to enhance or restore the size and shape of the breasts.

Breast examinations

Mammograms, breast physical examinations and breast self-examinations are the screening tests used to detect breast cancer and save many lives each year.

Breastfeeding

The practice of a woman feeding her infant with milk produced naturally by her breasts. The majority of women who receive breast implants are able to successfully breastfeed, though women who have a nipple incision are at greater risk for problems.

Breast implants

A silicone rubber shell filled with saline solution or silicone gel used in cosmetic or reconstructive breast surgery.

Breast lift

A procedure to lift and reshape sagging breasts. A breast lift can be performed in conjunction with a breast augmentation or breast reduction. Also known as a mastopexy.

Breast pocket

The 'pocket' created by the plastic surgeon in which to place the breast implant during breast augmentation surgery.

Breast reconstruction

Many different techniques are used to reconstruct a breast following a mastectomy or to correct breast deformities. Breast reconstruction techniques use either breast implants or a woman's own tissues to create a new, natural-looking breast.

Breast reduction

A procedure to reduce the size of large breasts. Breast reduction is performed for physical relief as well as for cosmetic reasons.

Capsular contracture

The most common complication of breast augmentation surgery, capsular contracture occurs when the scar capsule surrounding the breast implant shrinks and squeezes the implant. Surgical correction may be required in cases of very firm contraction.

Capsule

A scar capsule of dense fibrous connective tissue forms around any foreign object introduced into the body, in this case surrounding the breast implants.

Cleavage

The space between a woman's breasts, especially as revealed by clothing with a low neckline.

Consultation

Meeting you will have with a plastic surgeon prior to breast augmentation surgery.

Contralateral

Pertains to corresponding parts on the opposite sides of the body, such as referring to the left or right breast.

Cosmetic surgery

Surgery to improve one's appearance for aesthetic reasons, rather than for reasons of medical necessity.

Cup size

A measurement taken around the body, at the fullest point of the breasts to determine the cup size of a bra. Expressed as a letter that follows the band size to indicate the overall bra size, e.g. 42C.

Deflation/Rupture

Occurs when a breast implant leaks and is evidenced by a loss of size or change in shape of the affected breast. Saline leakage is not a health risk, though surgery to replace or remove the implant may be required.

DIEP flap breast reconstruction

A breast reconstruction method where skin from the lower abdomen is used to form a new, natural-looking breast.

Displacement

Occurs when breast implants move out of position. Larger movements, though uncommon, may require corrective surgery.

Dissection

To part tissue, such as during a medical procedure.

Expander implant

A temporary breast implant used during breast augmentation or breast reconstruction to stretch the breast tissue prior to placement of a permanent implant.

Infection

A complication of breast augmentation surgery that is uncommon but possible as with any surgery. Most infections experienced after breast augmentation surgery are mild and easily treated.

Informed consent

Informed consent documents communicate information about a surgical treatment and disclose risks and alternative treatments.

Internal mammary artery

Extends down either side of the sternum and gives off branches which supply blood to the breast. One of the two main sources of blood to the breasts (the other is the lateral thoracic artery).

In-patient surgery

A surgical procedure that requires the patient to stay in the hospital overnight.

Latissimus dorsi flap breast reconstruction

A breast reconstruction method where the latissimus dorsi, a muscle in the back, is brought around the body to the site of the breast.

Local anaesthesia

Form of anaesthesia which involves an injection to numb the area where an incision will be made during a surgical procedure.

Mammaplasty

A plastic surgery procedure performed on the breast, including breast augmentation, breast lift, breast reduction and breast reconstruction.

Mammary
Pertaining to the breast.

Mammogram/Mammography
A low-dose X-ray examination of the breast, mammograms are the best method for detecting early breast cancer and the only exam currently approved by the US Food and Drug Administration (FDA).

Mastectomy
The surgical removal of a breast, usually due to breast cancer. Many women who have had a mastectomy have benefitted from breast reconstruction as a means to restore their natural appearance.

Mastopexy
A procedure to lift and reshape sagging breasts. A mastopexy, or breast lift, can be performed in conjunction with breast augmentation or breast reduction.

Pectoralis major
The large chest muscle, commonly referred to as 'pecs', that supports the breasts and facilitates movements of the arms.

Pectoralis minor
Thin muscle of the upper chest that lies beneath the pectoralis major and connects the shoulder blade to the front of the ribs.

Periareolar incision
An incision used in breast augmentation surgery made at the perimeter of the areola. Also called the nipple incision.

Plastic surgery
Surgery intended to repair, restore or improve the body following trauma, injury or illness.

Pocket
The 'breast pocket' created by the plastic surgeon in which to place the breast implant during breast augmentation surgery.

Ptosis
Sagging or drooping of a body part, such as the breasts.

Reconstruction

Many different techniques are used to reconstruct a breast following a mastectomy or to correct breast deformities. Breast reconstruction techniques use either breast implants or a woman's own tissues to create a new, natural-looking breast.

Reduction

A procedure to reduce the size of large breasts. Breast reduction is performed for physical relief as well as for cosmetic reasons.

Regional anaesthesia

Form of anaesthesia where a 'region' of the body is anaesthetised without producing an unconscious state. A nerve block or an epidural administered during childbirth are examples.

Rippling

Indentions on the breast that are often caused by movement of the breast implant.

Rupture/Deflation

Occurs when a breast implant leaks and is evidenced by a loss of size or change in shape of the affected breast. Saline leakage is not a health risk, though surgery to replace or remove the implant may be required.

Saline

A solution made up of water and a small amount of salt. Breast implants are filled with saline solution after being inserted behind the breasts.

Scar

A mark left by healing tissue as part of the body's natural healing process. Scars left by breast augmentation surgery are usually small and well-hidden in the crease beneath the breast, around the nipple or in the armpit.

Scar capsule

A scar capsule of dense fibrous connective tissue forms around any foreign object introduced into the body, in this case surrounding the breast implants.

Sedation

Form of anaesthesia, usually administered via an injection, that reduces awareness but does not cause the patient to be unconscious.

Silicone elastomer
A type of silicone with elastic properties that is used to make the outer shell of breast implants, amongst other uses.

Silicone gel
A cohesive, gelatin-like substance that holds together uniformly while still retaining the natural give of breast tissue.

Sizer
A temporary, disposable breast implant used by the surgeon to test implant size, placement and fill level prior to replacement with the permanent implant.

Subglandular placement
Breast implants placed behind the mammary gland and in front of the pectoralis muscle. Subglandular placement is sometimes referred to as 'overs.'

Sub-muscular placement
Breast implants placed directly behind the pectoralis muscle. Sub-muscular placement is sometimes referred to as 'complete unders'.

Sub-pectoral placement
Breast implants placed with the upper two-thirds behind the pectoralis muscle. Sub-pectoral placement is sometimes referred to as 'partial unders'.

Tissue expander
An adjustable implant that can be inflated with saltwater to stretch the tissue at the mastectomy site to create a new tissue flap for implantation of the breast implant.

TRAM flap breast reconstruction
A breast reconstruction method where tissue from the transverse rectus abdominus, a muscle in the lower abdomen, is used to form a new, natural-looking breast.

Transaxillary incision

An incision used in breast augmentation surgery made in the armpit. Also called the armpit incision.

TUBA incision

An incision used in breast augmentation surgery made at the rim of the belly button.

Tubular breasts

A breast deformity where the breasts are underdeveloped and the areola appears stretched, resulting in a tubular-shaped breasts.

Ultrasound

A diagnostic imaging technique which uses high-frequency sound waves to create images of internal organs. Ultrasounds are used to examine breast abnormalities detected by breast cancer screening tests.

Help List

The British Association of Aesthetic Plastic Surgeons (BAAPS)

www.baaps.org.uk

The British Association of Plastic, Reconstructive and Aesthetic Surgeons (BAPRAS)

www.bapras.org.uk

The Care Quality Commission (CQC)

www.cqc.org.uk
Independent regulator of all health and social care services in England.

Medicines and Healthcare products Regulatory Agency (MHRA)

www.mhra.gov.uk
UK government agency which is responsible for ensuring medicines and medical devices are safe and work effectively.

Consumer Information

Consultingroom.com Ltd

www.consultingroom.com
The UK's largest and long-standing cosmetic surgery, non-surgical medical aesthetic and beauty treatment information website. Includes a directory of clinics in the UK and Ireland.

Consumer Health Information

Department of Health

www.dh.gov.uk

NetDoctor.co.uk

www.netdoctor.co.uk
Medical information and health website.

NHS

www.nhs.uk

Counselling Services

Counselling Directory

www.counselling-directory.org.uk
A website that lists counsellors and psychotherapists who are registered with a recognised professional body.

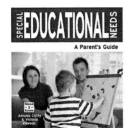

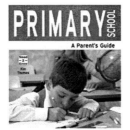
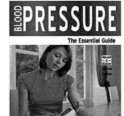
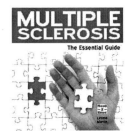